The *Heritage* *of American Catholicism*

A TWENTY-EIGHT-VOLUME SERIES DOCUMENTING THE HISTORY
OF AMERICA'S LARGEST RELIGIOUS DENOMINATION

EDITED BY

Timothy Walch

ASSOCIATE EDITOR
U.S. Catholic Historian

A Garland Series

"For God and Country:"

CATHOLIC SCHOOLING IN THE 1920s

FAYETTE BREAUX VEVERKA

Garland Publishing, Inc.
New York & London
1988

LIBRARY OF CONGRESS CATALOGING-IN-PUBLICATION DATA

Veverka, Fayette Breaux.
  For God and country: Catholic schooling in the 1920s / Fayette Breaux Veverka.
    p.   cm.--(Heritage of American Catholicism)
  Originally Presented as the Author's thesis (Ph. D.)--Columbia University, 1984.
  Bibliography: p.
  ISBN 0-8240-4101-1 (alk. paper)
    1. Catholic schools--United States--History--20th century. 2. Catholic Church--
Education--United States--History--20th century.
I. Title. II. Series.
LC501.V4 1988   88-9765
377'.82'73--dc19   CIP

DESIGN BY MARY BETH BRENNAN

PRINTED ON ACID-FREE, 250-YEAR-LIFE PAPER.
MANUFACTURED IN THE UNITED STATES OF AMERICA

ACKNOWLEDGEMENTS

I wish to take this opportunity to thank those who
have enriched my years of graduate study with their guidance
and wisdom. As a teacher and mentor at St. Louis University,
Malcolm L. Warford first stimulated my interest in American
cultural history. In his position as Director of Educational
Research at Union Theological Seminary, he continued to
encourage my historical studies and to demonstrate the
values of disciplined and critical inquiry. Now president
of Eden Theological Seminary, it is particularly fitting
that he graciously agreed to serve as chairman of my oral
defense committee. During my doctoral studies, I also
benefitted from the broad learning of my advisor, Philip H.
Phenix and the incisive questioning of Dwayne Huebner at
Teachers College. I am also indebted to Robert T. O'Gorman
of Scarritt College whose interest and work in the history
of Catholic schooling was crucial in the genesis of this
dissertation. I wish to thank Douglas Sloan, my dissertation sponsor for his encouragement in the development of
this study; William B. Kennedy at Union Theological
Seminary for his judicious criticisms as a member of my
dissertation committee; and Robert T. Handy, also from
Union, for serving as an examiner in the oral defense.
The final stages of work on the dissertation were completed
in the congenial and supportive atmosphere created by
my colleagues at the Institute of Religious Education and
Pastoral Ministry at Boston College.

No words can suffice to express my gratitude to my family, especially my parents, Otis and Fadrey Breaux, my husband, Jim and my son, Corey for their unfailing love and support that enabled me to persevere in this endeavor, sustaining me in ways they may never fully realize.

TABLE OF CONTENTS

INTRODUCTION

At the annual National Catholic Educational Association
(NCEA) convention held in New York City in April 1981, nearly
twenty thousand participants applauded sociologist James S.
Coleman's report comparing public and private high schools
in which he concluded that Roman Catholic schools more nearly
approximate the "common school" ideal of American education
than do public schools. Coleman was one among several
speakers addressing the convention theme, "Catholic Education:
A World of Difference."[1]

This event illustrates a fundamental ambiguity in the
nature of Catholic educational separatism in the United
States. There is substantial agreement among U.S. Catholics
that while Catholic schools are an important, and to some,
a necessary means for communicating a distinctively Catholic
worldview, they are at the same time genuinely American
institutions serving the public good. Underlying this
understanding of schooling is an assumption of the basic
compatibility between the demands of Catholic faith and
social life in the United States as well as the inseparability of the tasks of religious education and cultural
transmission. How is it, though, that leaders of an

[1]Coleman's complete study is published in High School
Achievement: Public, Catholic and Private Schools Compared
(New York: Basic Books, 1982).

educational enterprise that began as a reaction against
public schooling now boast of their accomplishments in
pursuit of goals that have historically been central to
the mission of public education? On what basis does
Catholic education justify its claim to uniqueness in view
of the admitted similarities between public and Catholic
school systems?

Furthermore, in spite of broad and fundamental agreement to support education which is both genuinely "Catholic"
and "American," it is clear that Catholics do not necessarily
agree on the meaning and implications of these twin commitments or the manner in which they are to be held together.
Critics argue that church-supported schools that serve as
an alternative to public schooling are socially divisive.
A policy of educational separatism has opened Catholics
to the charge of being "un-American," a bastion of educational
elitism, a haven for racial segregation, or a threat to
the existence of public schools. Among supporters of
Catholic schooling, there are those who are uneasy with
what they judge to be a facile identification of cultural
and religious values in the schools and an absence of a
critical and prophetic stance toward society. Some fear
the loss of a distinctive "Catholic" quality and presence
in the schools. Others argue against a "siege mentality"
in Catholic education and the perpetuation of an outdated
theology that prevents creative engagement with the realities of the modern world.

This educational debate is, of course, not new. As Catholics today wrestle with what it means educationally to be both "Catholic" and "American," we face what H. Richard Niebuhr described as "the enduring problem" of the proper relationship of Christian faith to human culture.[2] Current discussions regarding the religious and social functions of the school are at root efforts to discern the church's educationa identity and mission in the specific context of the U.S. in the 1980's. However, such a searching reappraisal demands an awareness of the historical roots of our inherited educational patterns and a critical evaluation of the values and assumptions underlying those educational policies and practices.

Toward this end, I propose in this dissertation to examine the evolution of Roman Catholic leaders' understanding of the church's relationship to U.S. society in the decade after World War I and the way in which this emerging self-consciousness influenced the development of Catholic school policy and practices at the beginning of what has been called the "ghetto period" in the U.S. Catholic experience.

Until recently, the ability of Catholic educators to penetrate the roots of their fundamental educational commitments and values has been limited by a narrowly institutional and ecclesiastic interpretation of U.S. Catholic educational history that presents educational

---

[2]Christ and Culture (New York: Harper & Row, 1951; Harper Torchbooks, 1956), p. 1.

policies and practices as the inevitable unfolding of the
official mandate of "every Catholic child in a Catholic
school" promulgated at the Third Plenary Council of Baltimore
in 1884. In this view, Catholic leaders had no other
choice but to pursue a policy of educational separatism to
protect U.S. Catholics from the Protestant, secular, or
anti-Catholic influences of the public school system.
Vincent P. Lannie has identified seven major themes domin-
ating this view of "Church and School Triumphant."

> 1. The triumphant progress of the Catholic
> Church in the United States in the face of
> incredible obstacles and the establishment of
> Catholic schools as an integral part of the
> Church's progress in America.
>
> 2. The essential compatibility of Roman
> Catholicism and American Republicanism. Hence
> an authentic American religious tradition is
> the Catholic religious tradition.
>
> 3. The equation of Catholic schooling with
> Catholic education.
>
> 4. The indispensability of the permeation theory
> for Catholic schooling, that is to say, the total
> environment educates in the classroom and school.
>
> 5. American public schools were not only anti-
> Catholic but incompatible with Catholic religious
> and educational convictions.
>
> 6. The development of a native Catholic journalism
> and literature as part of the Church's educational
> mission in the United States.
>
> 7. The evolution of a defensive structure and
> siege mentality in America.[3]

---

[3] "Church and School Triumphant: The Sources of American
Catholic Educational Historiography," History of Education
Quarterly 16 (Summer 1976):142.

This traditional interpretation of Catholic educational history minimizes discontinuities and conflicts in the evolution of Catholic schooling and fails to attend sufficiently to the complex interplay of social, cultural, economic and political forces shaping the development of Catholic educational strategies in this country.[4] More recent studies in Catholic educational, intellectual, social and cultural history have been shaped by a revisionist perspective that has helped American Catholics become more aware "of their real part in the historical process as an historical process" and not as the inevitable working out of a fixed and explicit blueprint determined in the distant past.[5] Robert Cross introduced this broader view in his analysis of the "Origins of the Catholic Parochial Schools in America" in which he shows that Catholics' commitment to a system of separate schooling evolved gradually in the course of the nineteenth century in response to a complex interplay of ideological, social, cultural and organizational factors within and outside the church and

[4] The historiography of public education and Protestant religious education has suffered from a similarly limited focus. For a discussion of these issues and alternative interpretations, see Lawrence A. Cremin, "A Note on Problematics and Sources," in Traditions of American Education (New York: Basic Books, 1976), pp. 129-163; Douglas Sloan, "Historiography and the History of Education," in Review of Research in Education, ed. Fred Kerlinger 1 (1973):239-69; and Robert W. Lynn, "The Uses of History: An Inquiry into the History of American Religious Education," Religious Education 67 (March-April 1972):83-97.

[5] Walter Ong, Frontiers in American Catholicism (New York: Macmillan, 1957), p. 9.

was not the result of some prior commitment to Catholic schooling as a normative ideal.[6]

Stimulated by Cross's insights and influenced by the revisionist historiographical approach to public education of Bernard Bailyn and Lawrence Cremin, recent historians of U.S. Catholicism have begun to examine education "in its elaborate intricate involvement with the rest of society."[7] At the forefront of this effort, Vincent P. Lannie proposes an approach which examines "the obvious and subtle features of the relationship between the Church as educator, the Catholic subculture and American society." This central focus, he argues, would reveal

> more extensive information about the variety
> of educational traditions within the Church,
> the diversity in the social identity of the
> Catholic laity and the institutional networks
> linking the immigrant to the broader American
> social order.[8]

Informed by this revisionist perspective, this study seeks to illumine the relationship of Catholics to American society at the beginning of the demise of "the immigrant church" in the decade following World War I and to analyze the manner in which the schools participated in this social and cultural transition. This analysis will be developed through

---

[6]Robert D. Cross, "The Origins of the Catholic Parochial Schools in America," _American Benedictine Review_ 16 (1965):194-209.

[7]Bernard Bailyn, _Education in the Forming of American Society: Needs and Opportunities for Research_ (New York: Vintage Books, 1960), p. 14.

[8]Vincent P. Lannie, "Catholic Educational Historiography in the Twentieth Century," Notre Dame, Indiana, n.d. (Mimeographed

an examination of the public positions and views of Catholic educators and church officials in positions of national leadership and influence on major policy questions affecting Catholic elementary and secondary schooling in the 1920's.

Specifically, the study will focus on discussions of the nature and purposes of Catholic schooling in American society, Catholic efforts to defend their schools from hostile critics and intrusive state and federal legislation, and the Catholic community's response to public demands for school standardization and teacher certification. It will deal only tangentially with instruction and ethos in the schools, curricular and pedagogical developments, and local implementation of policies supported by national educational leaders.

Two basic themes are interwoven in the narrative that follows: "ambiguity" and "Americanization," the former referring to the dynamic and contradictory character of the historical relationship of Roman Catholicism in the United States to its social and cultural context; the latter referring to the basic direction in which that dynamic has tended. This study argues that Catholic schools have historically exhibited what sociologist Thomas O'Dea has described as Catholicism's "simultaneous incorporation into and alienation from American culture."[9] In the 1920's this becomes particularly evident in disagreements among Catholic school leaders over an appropriate course of action with regard to issues such as standardization, teacher certification, and educational standards in the conduct of Catholic schools. However, as theoretical debates were

---

[9] American Catholic Dilemma (New York: Sheed & Ward, 1958; Mentor Omega Books, 1962), p. 71.

resolved into generally accepted policies and practices, Catholic
schooling reflects what educational historian Robert Lynn has
characterized as a "movement from alienation to accommodation"
in relation to the larger society. This study, then, is also a
description of the "Americanization" of Catholic schools: "a
consistent strain toward integration" of the education and ethos
in Catholic schools "with the larger social system"[10] revealed
in the decision of Catholic schools to adopt the forms, standards and procedures of public schools and an ideology that
maintained the identity of "American" and "Catholic" beliefs,
values, and ideals.

Beginning in the mid-nineteenth century and throughout the
first half of the twentieth, U.S. Catholics have been committed to
a separate system of schools as the primary means for carrying out
the church's educational mission. Since the Second Vatican Council
however, that commitment has been consistently challenged on theological, educational, economic, and sociological grounds. However,
much current debate over the continuing validity of Catholic
schools as an agency of religious education are often misconstrued
or misdirected as a result of either narrowly defined concepts
of the nature and purpose of Catholic religious education, or
overly simplistic understandings of the historical role of the
Catholic school system as a mediating institution where faith, culture and community come together in particular configurations to
create the unique "paideia" that lies at the heart of the U.S.
Catholic experience.[11] As yet we have insufficient

---

[10] Lynn, pp. 95-96.

[11] Lawrence A. Cremin develops the concepts of "educational
configurations" and "paideia" in the history of American education
in Public Education (New York: Basic Books, 1976) and Traditions
of American Education.

understanding of the complex historical factors that account for the institutional success of the Catholic school system, and little critical evaluation of the goals and purposes which the schools have served in the past and to which they should be directed in the future. The value of this study lies, in part, in its contribution to this on-going historical and critical task.

This study was conceived, in particular, to contribute to a much needed dialogue within the U.S. Catholic community between educators in the schools and those who identify themselves primarily as "religious educators" or "catechists," whether in school or parish settings. While sharing educational responsibilities in the church, these two groups today remain, to a large degree, socially, organizationally, and ideologically divided, without a common language to ground discussions of foundational educational concerns. This study attempts to help bridge this gap by identifying developments in Catholic schooling that contributed to the historical roots of this social split and by posing the question of the church's relation to culture as a central issue that challenges school educators to explore the religious dimensions of their tasks and religious educators to view their role within a broadly educational context in carrying out the church's educational mission.

Chapter I

THE AMBIGUITY OF CATHOLIC EDUCATIONAL SEPARATISM

The Two Spirits of American Catholicism

As Robert O'Gorman has argued in his study of "The
Catholic Church's Educational Mission and Ministry in the
U.S.A.,"

> the position on Christianity-culture relation-
> ship as elaborated in the two centuries old
> experience of the American Catholic Church
> has not been a unitary one. Instead, it has
> been expressed in an ambivalent manner.[1]

Apprehensive of the perils, yet hopeful about the promises
of the U.S. experiment, Catholics have had particular reason
to view their society with mixed feelings. Experiences of
religious persecution, nativist bigotry, and abject poverty
in urban slums fostered among Catholics a deep suspicion of
and alienation from Protestant, Anglo-Saxon culture. On
the other hand, a republican form of government with guaran-
tees of civil and religious liberties coupled with the
economic opportunities of a relatively open society was an
enormous attraction to Catholic immigrants suffering from religious, political and economic oppression in Europe. These
polar attitudes, operating with somewhat different effect on
various levels of social, cultural and institutional life
have contributed to what O'Gorman has referred to as "the two
spirits of American Catholicism."

----

[1](Ph.D. dissertation, University of Notre Dame, 1977),
pp. 55-56.

One stream in the American Catholic tradition has roots in the experiences and reflections of a small, aristocratic English Catholic minority in the colonies around the time of the American Revolution. Under the leadership of Lord Baltimore in 1634, Catholics established in Maryland the first government in modern times to grant toleration to all Christian denominations. Although Protestant distrust, hostility and suspicion were codified in legal restrictions against Catholicism throughout the colonies, these Catholics shared English cultural traditions and their social and economic status was secure. This facilitated a generally optimistic and positive outlook in the Catholic community about the eventual accommodation of the faith to its American environment. To an extent that was rare in the subsequent experiences of a church preoccupied with a burgeoning immigrant population, Catholic life and thought in Maryland was notably open to the influences of its environment.

Catholic religious understanding in this context was characterized by an "acceptance and promotion of religious liberty within a framework of accepted religious pluralism."[2] This view reflected the influence of Enlightenment thought, in particular, Lockean political philosophy on Catholic theology. John Carroll, the first American Catholic bishop, was the leading spokesperson in an effort

---

[2] James Hennesey, "Roman Catholic Theology in the United States," _Louvain Studies_ 6 (September 1976):12.

> to articulate a positive religious vision
> which could be reconciled with the acceptance
> of scientific criticism, the existence of
> religious pluralism, the advocacy of consti-
> tutionalism, and a definition of the person
> which stressed individual reason.

Carroll's thought was a synthesis of Enlightenment humanism with the Augustinian tradition of the unity of nature and grace that characterized the church's medieval synthesis and "enabled the Church both to accept and critically to address cultural developments."[3] He emphasized the dynamic, living presence of the Holy Spirit in persons and the rights of individual conscience. His theological arguments were appeals to reason and experience rather than to authority or metaphysical principles.

Another significant aspect of his leadership was his firm belief in the "legitimacy of national expression in the forms, structures and thought of the Catholic body."[4] His "Americanizing" influence was evident in his resistance to Roman influence in U.S. church affairs, his acceptance of the separation of church and state in the U.S., his successful bid to have clergy in the U.S. elect their first bishop, his consultative and collegial administrative style, and his advocacy of lay participation in the selection of pastors and a vernacular liturgy.

---

[3]Joseph Chinnici, "Politics and Theology: From Enlightenment Catholicism to the Condemnation of Americanism," Working Paper Series, Center for the Study of American Catholicism, Series 9, no. 3 (Notre Dame, Indiana: University of Notre Dame, Spring 1981), pp. 3, 10.

[4]Hennesey, p. 12

This irenic and conciliatory approach to culture in the eighteenth century was not to remain dominant in the American Catholic experience. Though never entirely submerged, and vigorously reasserted in the liberal views of the "Americanizers" in the last third of the nineteenth century, this spirit of accommodation was overshadowed by a spirit of hostility and defensiveness toward the world stemming from two main sources in the nineteenth century: 1) the reactionary stance of the church in Rome toward the social and cultural upheavals in Europe; and 2) the experience of mass immigration that transformed the shape of American Catholicism.

From the time of the French Revolution giving birth to the secular state through the loss of the papal states in 1870, the traditional power, prestige and status of the Roman Catholic Church as an arbiter of culture was severely threatened by the forces of nationalism, liberal political theory, and intellectual and philosophical modernism.

> In the face of these confusing developments, the prevailing confidence of eighteenth-century Catholicism gave way to fear and suspicion. Catholics began to demand greater vigilance in distinguishing and defending the City of God from the City of Man.[5]

Though some liberals in the church urged Catholic rapprochement with the tendencies of the modern age,

---

[5]Robert D. Cross, The Emergence of Liberal Catholicism in America (Cambridge: Harvard University Press, 1958; reprint ed., Chicago: Quadrangle Paperback, 1968), p. 2.

conservatives carried the day, urging staunch defense against
even the slightest compromise. To strengthen the authority
and power of the church, conservatives orchestrated the increased centralization of the church under the papacy; and
to the rationalist and secular spirit of the age, churchmen
responded with a renewed stress on other-worldly devotional
piety. These two central tendencies found expression in
three declarations of the pontificate of Pius IX which together constituted the church's "ultimatum to the world."[6]
Ineffabilis Deus in 1854 proclaimed as dogma the Immaculate
Conception of Mary. In 1864, the Syllabus of Errors addressed
what Rome judged to be "the principle errors of our time,"
most prominently, the belief that "the Roman Pontiff can
and ought to reconcile himself to, and agree with progress,
liberalism, and modern civilization."[7] Finally, the declaration of papal infallibility at the Vatican Council served
to confirm the ultramontanist character of the church in
the last quarter of the nineteenth century.

Until the late nineteenth century when Rome intervened
more directly in U.S. church affairs, these developments
in the church universal provided the backdrop and source
of ideological support for events having more immediate

---

[6]Emmet John Hughes, The Church and Liberal Society,
cited by O'Gorman, p. 58.

[7]Cross, Emergence, p. 16.

effect on the growth of a defensive spirit within U.S. Catholicism.

The mid-nineteenth century was a period of radical transformation in the character, ethos, and structure of the Catholic Church in the United States brought about by the massive immigration of first Irish, then German Catholics. The population figures alone give some indication of the extent to which the Catholic body was changing. In 1815, there were fewer than 200,000 Catholics in the U.S. composing "chiefly an Anglo-American minority . . . culturally an American group."[8] By 1865, immigration had swollen the Catholic population to 3.5 million, making it the largest single denomination in the U.S. That figure nearly doubled to six million by 1880.

This influx of mostly indigent, non-English, non-Protestant cultural groups threatened the stability of a heretofore relatively homogeneous society. "Essentially, Americans thought of Catholics as aliens."[9] Citizens feared a "barbarian invasion" of "the very scum and dregs of human nature"[10] whose lack of education, experience and understanding

---

[8]Jay Dolan, "A Critical Period in American Catholicism," The Review of Politics 35 (October 1973):523.

[9]Robert D. Cross, "The Changing Image of the City Among American Catholics," Catholic Historical Review 48 (April 1962):563.

[10]Allan Nevins and Milton H. Thomas, eds., The Diary of George Templeton Strong, 1835-1875, cited by Vincent P. Lannie, "The Emergence of Catholic Education in America," Notre Dame Journal of Education 3 (Winter 1973):297.

made them particularly ill-suited for effective participation in a democratic society with a republican form of government.

Immigrants were also suspect because of their religious allegiances. In 1835, Samuel F. B. Morse warned "that there is good reason for believing that the despots of Europe are attempting by the spread of Popery in this country, to subvert its free institutions." In apocalyptic terms, Morse predicted that the "question of Popery and Protestantism, or Absolutism and Republicanism is fast becoming and will shortly be the GREAT, ABSORBING QUESTION, not only of this country but of the whole civilized world."[11] Nativist hostility was expressed in economic, political and social discrimination against the immigrant, physical isolation in the slum wards of major cities, and physical violence and the destruction of church property in urban riots.

However, Protestants made no serious attempt to prohibit immigration because of America's need for a labor force to fuel the fires of industrial expansion, as well as their faith in the power of American institutions to transform the foreigner.[12] Middle class citizens supported efforts to "uplift" and "improve" the immigrant through the socializing influence of the public schools and

---

[11]Ibid., p. 298.

[12]Cross, "Changing Image," pp. 562-75.

legislative measures to impose temperance, compulsory education and women's rights. Immigrant communities often resented what appeared to them as cultural and class imposition and continued to cultivate Protestant fears by their ultramontanism, other-worldly devotional piety, and foreign cultural ties.[13]

Thus, cultural and religious alienation in America was the most immediate source of the separatist spirit that came to dominate the ethos of the Catholic Church in the U.S. through the nineteenth century.

> Hostile to the Protestant majority, suspicious of governmental enterprise, and averse to the active, melioristic spirit of the times, these Catholics met secular culture so far as possible only on their own terms. Their Catholicism was the symbol as well as the seal of their separation from the culture. Like their ultramontane counterparts in Europe, they opposed all innovations except those that would obviously strengthen the defensive armor of the Church against the age.[14]

One of the primary innovations growing out of this defensive mentality was an undertaking without parallel in the history of the church: the creation of a Catholic parochial school system.

---

[13]Ibid. See also William Greenbaum, "America in Search of a New Ideal: An Essay on the Rise of Pluralism," Harvard Educational Review 44 (August 1974):411-40.

[14]Cross, Emergence, p. 25.

The Defensive Spirit and Educational Separatism

Immigration and the consequent expansion of U.S.
Catholicism brought changes to both church and society that
demanded a redefinition and rearrangement of configurations
of religion, education and culture. In one sense, both
church and state faced the same basic problem: unity within
diversity. How was the church to form "a Catholic people"
with communities treasuring different cultural and national
expressions of their faith? How was a nation founded upon
a peculiarly Protestant religious vision to sustain its
way of life in the face of "foreign invaders" whose social
values, religious faith and national loyalties seemed to
threaten the very fabric of American life? In response to
these challenges, both state and church turned to education
as a solution.

The common school movement grew out of the conviction
that in the face of rapid social change, education could
no longer be left to informal socialization processes
and that the adequate preparation of citizens for social,
economic and political life required formal schooling for
all youth. As an advocate and spokesman for public schooling, Horace Mann recognized that a major obstacle to gathering support for the cause was the issue of religion in the
common schools. By 1840 legal separation of church and

state had been achieved on both federal and state levels, effectively excluding denominational instruction in the common schools. However, most Christian denominations rejected the notion that moral education could occur without the support of religion. Mann's solution to this dilemma was to eliminate "sectarian" forms of religious instruction while retaining a non-denominational approach that taught the "common core of all religions," in particular, through the reading of the Bible without comment.

Though initially unopposed to the common school movement, Catholics were vehemently opposed to this resolution of the problem of religion in education. The experiences of Catholic children forced to use the Protestant version of the Bible, to study from explicitly anti-Catholic textbooks, to worship using Protestant hymns and prayers, and to endure religious and ethnic insults from insensitive teachers convinced many Catholics that Mann's "non-denominational religion" was, in fact, Protestant. Fearful that such schools posed a threat to the immigrant's faith, John Hughes, the militant Irish bishop of New York expressed the concern of the Catholic leadership in the 1840's when he declared flatly that "in our age the question of education is the question of the church."[15] The failure of repeated efforts to remove offensive elements from the

---

[15]Cited by Jay P. Dolan, The Immigrant Church
Baltimore, Maryland: Johns Hopkins University Press, 1975), p. 100.

public schools convinced many Catholics of the need to establish their own schools to protect the faith of their children from this Protestant influence, to guard against the religious indifference they feared would result in a religiously pluralistic country, and to preserve a Catholic perspective in the teaching of secular subjects.[16]

As the public schools became increasingly secularized, to some extent as the result of their own efforts to eliminate explicitly Protestant practices from the schools, Catholics were still critical. Catholics in the U.S. had come to view the separation of church and state as a providential safeguard, given the minority status of Catholicism in a Protestant country. Nevertheless, the separation of religion from education was another matter entirely. The underlying issue in the view of the Catholic hierarchy was the control of education. Feeling besieged from without and fearful of fragmentation within, their primary goal was to preserve the immigrant's loyalty to the church, and they were unwilling to trust the power of universal schooling in the hands of either the Protestant majority or the secular state. John Hughes' call to build the school before the church was in part a move to maintain the pre-eminent authority of church over against the competing claims of the state.

[16]M. C. Klinkhammer, "Historical Reasons for the Inception of the Parochial School System," Catholic Education Review 52 (February 1954):93-94 (Hereafter cited as CER).

Many immigrants objected to the public schools on cultural, as well as strictly religious grounds. To social and cultural elites, one of Mann's most persuasive arguments in support of public schools was their power to assimilate and "Americanize" the foreigner, the indigent and those classes of people who would otherwise threaten the stability of a homogeneous society. Typically, public school educators saw their task as the assimilation of immigrants into the Anglo-Saxon tradition. As one Chicago public school administrator insisted, cultural differences were to be "minimized, obliterated, homogenized in the process of unification."[17] In a study of the education of Catholics in Chicago, James Sanders found that

> Catholic ethnics, most of them Celtic, Germanic, Slavic, or Latin origin, found the public schools of Chicago generously endowed with a distasteful Anglo-Saxon flavor that represented American public education's typical response to its mandate for Americanizing the immigrant child. The curriculum, the textbooks, and, most importantly, the teachers tended to impress a single mold rooted in the English language as the only legitimate medium of expression, English literature and history as essential to the American experience, and Anglo-Saxon virtue as the foundation of national character.[18]

Successive waves of immigration through the nineteenth and early twentieth century brought Irish, German, and then

---

[17]Cited by James W. Sanders, The Education of an Urban Minority: Catholics in Chicago, 1833-1965 (New York: Oxford University Press, 1977), p. 40.

[18]Ibid.

southern and eastern Europeans who clearly wanted to maintain their ties with the old country and who resented
the implication that to do so was somehow "un-American."

> Though most immigrants agreed that their
> children must be trained in the 'American
> experience' and even . . . that the 'essen-
> tial purpose of the American school system
> is to form American citizens,' but they did
> not see what that had to do with the 'Anglo-
> Saxon tradition.' The immigrant found nothing
> in the 'ideas and traditions' of his home
> 'utterly opposed to the requirements of Ameri-
> can citizenship.' He resented the implications
> that in the public school his social customs
> would be 'minimized' and 'obliterated.' Why
> could he not be an American and remain Irish
> or Polish or German, too?[19]

It was this intransigence on the part of public education to
ethnic values and sensibilities that alienated large groups
of immigrants and encouraged them to establish their own
schools where the unity of faith and cultural traditions
would be honored rather than scorned.

Religious and cultural alienation coupled with the
church's inability to exert much influence on the shape
of public education served to reinforce a perception of
the basic antagonism of Catholicism and Americanism for
many nineteenth century Catholics. Catholic schools became "the educational rampart of the defensive structure
of American Catholicism."[20]

---

[19]Ibid., p. 41

[20]Vincent P. Lannie, "The Teaching of Values in
Public, Sunday and Catholic Schools: An Historical Perspective," Religious Education 70 (March-April 1975):135.

Catholics felt themselves suffocated in
a hostile society and gradually developed a
religious and cultural separatism to go along
with their physical ghettos in the slum wards
of the cities. Constant rejection of their
demands caused a growing intransigence on
their part and a caustic suspicion, sometimes
conscious, sometimes unconscious of the society
with all of its perils and humiliations. When
the schools appeared to them to be as intract-
able as the rest of society, Catholics scorned
them in the same way. Thus the gradual development of a system of parochial schools that would
protect the religiosity and ethnicity of Catholic
children and reinforce the positive self-identity
of church and home. Catholic cries of godless
and secularistic public education only hastened
the development of their own schools.[21]

Although most accounts of the origins of the Catholic

school system in the U.S. emphasize their roots in the

church's "ghetto mentality," the story would be incomplete

without serious attention to the social diversity within

the Catholic population, including those seeking some recon-

ciliation between Catholic faith and American nationality,

and the effect of such views on the development of educa-

tional policy.

The Accommodationist Spirit and Catholic Schools

Thomas T. McAvoy has insisted that

to attempt to point to any national characteristic of the Catholics of the nineteenth
century in the United States, outside of a
reverent loyalty to the Pope, one would be
confined almost entirely to those principles

---

[21]Idem, "Emergence," p. 309.

of faith and morals which constitute the
religious bases of Catholicism.[22]

In their social views in particular, Catholics held diverse

understandings of the manner in which Catholicism should

relate to American life.

   Though there were few apologists to advocate an inte-

gration of Catholicism and American culture before the

"emergence of liberal Catholicism" in the last third of

the nineteenth century, a spirit of accommodation within

the immigrant population provided a counterpoint to the

isolationist thrust of conservative Catholic life and thought.

>   The immigrant invasion had never been one
> homogeneous mass of uncultured, indigent,
> famine-driven peasants. Some had emigrated
> well fortified by intellectual training or
> experience in urban, industrial life against
> the insecurity of American experience. They
> were able to adapt themselves to free compe-
> tition in religion as well as economics, and
> to recognize that all non-Catholics did not
> act like anti-Catholics. Others brought to
> America the professional status, manual skill
> or financial resources which enabled them to
> win economic and social independence relatively
> simply and rapidly. Because they were not
> so readily coerced by American society, they
> were less likely to resist it as strenuously,
> and more apt to recognize the great opportuni-
> ties America offered to the enterprising individ-
> ual. They were, in short, more readily accultu-
> rated.[23]

Whether suspicious of their new environment and pro-

tective of their Old World ties, or confident and eager to

---

[22]"The American Catholic Minority in the Later
Nineteenth Century," Review of Politics 15 (1953):279.

[23]Cross, Emergence, p. 29.

take advantage of the opportunities of an open society,
immigrants turned to education as a vehicle for forging
a new sense of economic, communal and civic identity in
the United States.

> Behind the concern for learning lay three
> interlocking motives. The most explicit in
> their literature and also most deeply rooted
> in Old World experience was simply the de-
> sire to earn a better living, and, if possible,
> to gain both riches and fame. The second, and
> the one which seems to have been most promin-
> ent in religious congregations in America,
> was the need to shape a structure of family
> and communal life which would fit the require-
> ments of mobile and urban existence. The
> third was specifically ethnic: the quest of a
> definition of national identity which would
> fulfill the sense of duty to their homeland
> or to their people that memory inspired and
> still not contradict their new allegiance to
> America.[24]

Confronted with a choice between public and parochial schools,
Catholics' decisions depended to a large extent on their
judgments of the effectiveness of either system to respond
to this complex configuration of social aspirations. To
the extent that these aspirations differed, so too did
their educational choices.

Most Catholics throughout the nineteenth century
either tolerated, accepted, or positively supported public
school education for their children. In part, Catholic
schools served only a minority of Catholics because of
the inability of the church to provide sufficient educational

---

[24]Timothy L. Smith, "Immigrant Social Aspirations
and American Education, 1880-1930," American Quarterly 21
(1969):525.

facilities and staff to keep up with rapid population growth.
However, other, more positive reasons also motivated
Catholics to support public schools. In heavily Catholic
urban areas where public schools were staffed largely
with Catholic teachers and Catholics sat on commissions
and boards that supervised the operations of the schools,
most parents saw little danger to their children's faith
in these community schools. Many priests, often themselves
a product of public education, found no objection to public
schools which did not discriminate against Catholicism.[25]

In addition to being unconvinced of the danger of
public schools, many Catholics were sincerely opposed to
the idea of parish schools. A prominent convert to
Catholicism and an early opponent of parochial schools
(although he later changed his position to support the
idea), Orestes Brownson feared that such schools fostered
an undesirable separatist mentality among American Catholics.[26]
A few socially radical clergy such as New York priest
Edward McGlynn argued that instead of creating schools,

---

[25]The initial reluctance of Catholics to support
parochial schools has been noted by Donna Merwick, Boston
Priests 1848-1910: A Study of Social and Intellectual Change
(Cambridge, Massachusetts: Harvard University Press, 1973),
pp. 88-89; Howard Ralph Weisz, "Irish American and Italian
American Educational Views and Activities, 1870-1900: A
Comparison," (Ph.D. dissertation, Columbia University, 1968),
pp. 161-62; and Dolan, Immigrant Church, p. 109.

[26]Dolan, Immigrant Church, p. 109.

the church's limited resources should be committed to more urgent religious and social needs.[27]   Boston's Archbishop Williams felt that the good of the church in America was best served by maintaining cordial relationships with Protestant leaders. He predicted that in Boston, "severance from American Protestant institutions would destroy the whole social and religious fabric of the growing city," and for this reason opposed parochial schools.[28]   Finally, the heavy financial burden of supporting a parallel system of Catholic schools with the meager resources of an immigrant people was a major obstacle disturbing both clergy and laity alike.

Finally, many immigrants simply saw greater educational, economic and social advantages in sending their children to public schools. Public schools often were able to deliver a higher quality of education than the parochial schools and they were free. In the socially and religiously mixed public schools, Catholic students had the opportunity to cultivate friendships and gain confidence in dealing with the "non-Catholic" world that often proved beneficial in gaining status and respectability in the larger community.

---

[27]Robert Emmett Curran, "Edward McGlynn, the Social Question and the Spectre of Schism," in Michael Augustine Corrigan and the Shaping of Conservative Catholicism in America, 1878-1902 (New York: Arno Press, 1978).

[28]Merwick, p. 70.

As one conservative accusingly noted, these Catholics "were willing to risk the religious defects of the public schools in order to get cultural benefits."[29] For immigrants eager to see their children integrated into American society, the public schools offered the surest route to Americanization.

The accommodationist spirit, however, was not limited to those Catholics who chose a public school education for their children. The choice of Irish and German immigrants to support Catholic schools reflected religious and cultural objections to the public schools, but did not necessarily imply a desire to remain completely isolated from American life. Though it has become the institutional symbol of Catholic defensiveness, many immigrants viewed the parish school not so much as a fortress, but a bridge between two different cultures. As Mary Perkins Ryan has observed:

> The parochial school at that period served to slow up the process of acculturation, to make it less of a traumatic experience--less of a complete, almost instantaneous break with the European past and all it stood for. The children in the Catholic schools were 'Americanized'--but by teachers of their own race and religion, who clung in great part to old ways, only slowly adopting the new.[30]

---

[29]Cross, Emergence, p. 137.

[30]Are Parochial Schools the Answer? Catholic Education in the Light of the Council (New York: Holt, Rinehart & Winston, 1963), p. 37.

To say that the school served as a mediator between cultures means that in the process of integrating immigrants' economic, religious, civic, and ethnic aspirations, the schools expressed elements of both conservation and transformation, of isolation and accommodation. On the one hand, the church's concern to preserve a distinctive Catholic culture and to insure the loyalty and obedience of Catholics to the authority of the church was met by religious teaching that emphasized Catholicism as the one true fount of salvation, catechisms that reinforced the uniformity of doctrinal teaching, textbooks that offered "Catholic" interpretations of both European and U.S. history, and teaching personnel who were members of religious orders.[31] The immigrant's desire to resist assimilation and maintain a distinct cultural identity resulted in a pattern of school organization along ethnic lines which supported, in some cases, the teaching of foreign languages, history and customs.[32] In these ways, Catholic schools differed from their public school counterparts and expressed the defensive posture of the schools.

On the other hand, as Howard Weisz noted,

The parish schools came into existence not only to further the Catholic faith, but

---

[31]O'Gorman, pp. 123-28 and Dolan, Immigrant Church, pp. 110-20.

[32]Sanders, Education of an Urban Minority, p. 45.

> also to serve as a surrogate for the pub-
> lic schools,

and despite an ideology of non-compromise with its environment,

> the direction of change was to bring the
> parochial schools closer to the public
> schools. The dream of creating a pure
> Catholic culture on the base of the
> parochial schools was doomed.[33]

By the 1870's an increasingly assimilated Irish com-
munity emphasized the "Americanizing" function of their
English-language schools. Patrick Ford, editor of the
Irish World, insisted that Catholics wanted

> no foreign schools with doctrines, ideas,
> and methods at variance with our consti-
> tutional principles, disturbing, instead
> of conserving national harmony.

Fidelity to both Catholic traditions and American nationality
became hallmarks of such schools. As one New York priest
declared in defending the patriotism of his parish school:

> We have no flag but the stars and stripes,
> which we fly on every public occasion over
> school and rectory, speak no other language
> than United States, and when we sing you
> can always hear Hail Columbia, America, the
> Star Spangled Banner, etc.[34]

Pressure from parents to emulate the public schools
caused shifts in the curriculum and organization of parochial
schools. In order for Catholic students to meet state entrance

---

[33]"Irish-American Attitudes and the Americanization
of the English Language Parochial School," New York History
5 (1972):175.

[34]Ibid., pp. 159-60.

requirements for public high schools, parochial schools
were obliged to follow the curriculum of public elementary
schools closely. In addition, public school teaching was
a popular occupation for young Catholic women. Their
skills and training had to be comparable to public school
graduates.[35]

A comparison of public and parochial courses of study
reveals many basic similarities. In an examination of nineteenth century Catholic textbooks, Timothy Walch concluded
that "the overwhelming majority of Catholic schoolbooks were
in complete thematic agreement with their public school counterparts." In particular Walch found that both public and
Catholic school texts emphasized the educational value of
nature, a conservative code of social values such as industry, piety, deference, thrift, honest, and diligence;
and finally, patriotism and the superiority of the United
States to other nations.[36] In many secular subjects like
spelling and grammar, parochial schools used texts that
were also popular in public schools.[37]

Fear of losing support to public schools motivated
Catholic school leaders to see parochial schools as

<hr>

[35]Ibid., p. 170

[36]"Catholic Schoolbooks and American Values,"
Religious Education 73 (September-October 1978):582-91.

[37]Dolan, Immigrant Church, p. 113.

competitive with, rather than simply an alternative to
public schools. As public schools expanded their curriculum
and moved toward greater systematization, centralization,
and professionalization, Catholic schools had little choice
but to make similar efforts.

Baltimore Council Affirms Separatism

The Catholic hierarchy's commitment to a policy of
educational separatism at the Third Plenary Council in
Baltimore in 1884 represented only a partial resolution to
the problem of religion and culture for the U.S. church.
Council legislation requiring every Catholic parish to
maintain a parochial school and Catholic parents to send
their children to these schools certainly reinforced the
isolationist structure of Catholic educational strategy.
However, as the above analysis has tried to demonstrate,
supporters of Catholic schools did not share a single set
of assumptions about the relationship between Catholicism
and American life. Rather, the schools were able to suc-
ceed because they became a vehicle for somewhat differently
conceived ends. The lack of coordination and relative
autonomy of Catholic schools (described in the Catholic
Review in 1881 as "little more than a congeries of fortuitous
atoms"[38]) enabled the schools to more or less respond to
the desires of Germans to preserve their language and

---

[38]Cited in Weisz, "Irish-American Attitudes," p. 167.

customs, the social ambitions of the Irish to be Americanized, the concerns of theological conservatives to maintain
a pure Catholic culture, and the goal of many clergy and
bishops to maintain episcopal authority by encouraging
the dependency of the laity.

The Council sought to accommodate some of these
ideological and regional differences by reserving decisions
on the enforcement of these strictures and the discern-
ment as to what properly constitutes a Catholic school to
the judgment of the local bishop. This modicum of flexi-
bility written into the official school policy allowed
renewed challenges to educational separatism to re-emerge
in the late nineteenth century. Commitment to a policy of
educational separatism had not resolved the deeper social
and cultural issues that were a source of increasing tensions between conservatives and liberals in the church.

The Americanizers' Challenge

After the Civil War, despite continual efforts by
church leaders to preserve unity and harmony among American
Catholics, conservatives and liberals clashed in a series
of disputes creating what has been called "the great crisis
in American Catholic history."[39] One major area of controversy
centered on the social functions of Catholic schooling.

---

[39]Thomas T. McAvoy, The Great Crisis in American Catholic
History, 1895-1900 (Chicago: Regnery, 1957).

In what Robert Cross has referred to as "the emergence
of liberal Catholicism," articulate spokesmen such as
Cardinal James Gibbons, John Keane, Bishop John Spalding,
and Archbishop John Ireland argued for a greater openness
to and engagement with American society. Their liberal
agenda included efforts to make state-controlled education
more responsive to Catholic concerns, thus lessening the
need for a parallel Catholic system of schooling. Their
efforts were suspect to many--both Catholics and Protestants--
who saw no acceptable compromise between church and state-
sponsored education.

Allied with theological conservatives, German Catholics
became leading opponents of Americanization. Assuming
leadership in the movement to establish and maintain Catholic
schools after the Civil War, German communities saw the
schools as a vital part of their effort to preserve the
language, traditions and customs of parish life in the Old
World.

> Fresh from Germany and feeling isolated
> because of their language differences, the
> German Catholics in the United States from
> the outset insisted that separate churches
> were an absolute necessity for themselves.
> The German Catholics settled together in
> colonies whenever possible, often by their
> own choice, more often under the direction
> of a zealous priest or missionary. They
> desired to have churches [and schools] in
> which their traditional religious observances
> and customs would be carried out, where they
> could hear sermons in their mother tongue,
> go to confession as they had learned to con-
> fess from early childhood, and take an active

part in parish life through their beloved
societies. They wanted the order and disci-
pline of parish life as they had known it
before coming to the United States.[40]

Religious leaders recognized that for the German immigrant,
"love of God and the love of the fatherland were mystically
united." They were convinced that if the immigrants "could
not practice their faith in the German way when they came to
America, then they would not practice their faith at all."[41]
Conservatives in the church whose main concern was preserving the immigrants' faith against the dangers of American
life were convinced by these arguments and opposed a too
hasty process of Americanization in which the loss of German
language and traditions seemed sure to result in losses to
the faith.

Ethnicity, then, was a key factor in the debate over
Americanization. It is not surprising that church leaders
urging the accommodation of the church to the modern world
were virtually all Irish, with the notable exception of
John Spalding whose roots went back to the early English
Catholic settlers of Maryland. Sharing English cultural
traditions, Anglo-Catholics had little difficulty in
reconciling their faith with American citizenship and
functioned as a link between immigrant Catholics of Irish,

---

[40]Coleman J. Barry, The Catholic Church and the
German Americans (Milwaukee: Bruce, 1953), p. 9.

[41]Ibid.

German and French nationality and U.S. culture.[42] The
Irish who arrived in massive numbers before the Civil War
assumed leadership of the church in America. Their
knowledge of the English language, the absence of strong
Irish cultural traditions, and their identification with
America as a symbol of successful resistance to British
oppression under which they had suffered in Ireland--all
facilitated a more ready assimilation into American society
than other ethnic groups. By the time of peak German
immigration in the 1880's, many second generation Irish
and well-established English Catholics were at home in
America, and unlike their German co-religionists, saw few
reasons to remain cautious and suspicious of their cultural
context.

The liberal cause took on greater urgency when the
combined effects of the educational legislation of the
Third Plenary Council along with the influx of massive
numbers of German Catholic immigrants intent on preserving
their language and culture served to inflame renewed
nativist hostilities toward Catholicism in the 1880's and
90's.[43] Protestant charges that Catholicism was essentially
a foreign element on the U.S. scene reinforced the liberals'
conviction that the church's future vitality depended on

---

[42]This theme is developed by Thomas T. McAvoy, A
History of the Catholic Church in the United States (Notre
Dame, Indiana: University of Notre Dame Press, 1969).

[43]See John Higham, Strangers in the Land: Patterns of
American Nativism 1860-1925 (New York: Atheneum, 1968).

its ability to become fully Americanized. Archbishop John Ireland of Minnesota was by the far the most voluble and controversial figure among the Americanizers. He undertook what amounted to a crusade to convince the American church of his vision.

> Church and age! Unite them in the name of
> humanity, in the name of God. Church and
> age! They pulsate alike; the God of nature
> works in one, the God of supernatural revela-
> tion works in the other--in both the self-same
> God.[44]

He specifically addressed many of his arguments to German Catholics. In an address before a German audience in 1888, he urged Germans to teach their children English so as to enable them to participate and contribute to the political and business life of the country. Toward the end of his speech, he articulated his vision of Americanization.

> What I do mean by Americanization is the
> filling up of the heart with love for America
> and for her institutions. It is the harmon-
> izing of ourselves with our surroundings, so
> that we will be as to the manner born, and
> not as strangers in a strange land, caring
> apparently but slightly for it, and entitled
> to receive from it but meagre favors. It is
> the knowing of the language of the land and
> failing in nothing to prove our attachment to
> our laws, and our willingness to adopt, as
> dutiful citizens, all that is good and laud-
> able in its social life and civilizations . .
> . . I am sure I speak in the name of the
> children of the Church in America, and I
> tell their truest thoughts, when I proclaim
> that they are to the core Americans in love
> and loyalty, and that they deem it highest
> honor to be and to be called Americans. And
> why not? Has it not been to their gain that

---

[44]Cited in Curran, p. 490.

Catholics have passed from other lands to
America? Have they not here as nowhere else,
rewards for thrift and industry? Have they
not here, as nowhere else, liberty? Is not
the Church in America free, as nowhere else,
to work and to grow, and to shed around her
the benign influence of truth and grace? He
who does not feel all this, and does not thank
God that he is an American, should in simple
consistency betake his foreign soul to foreign
shores, and crouch in misery and abjection be-
neath tyranny's sceptre.[45]

Given these convictions, Ireland saw a need for an
alternative to both secular public schools and separate
parochial schools. In a speech before the 1890 National
Educational Association convention, Ireland urged a rapprochement between private and public educational efforts. He
praised state schools and acknowledged their right to educate. He argued that it was only the continued neglect of
religion in the public school curriculum that created a
need for separate church schools. To remedy this situation, Ireland proposed that the state erect a system of
denominational schools and pay only for the secular instruction it offered. Another alternative, he suggested, would
be for the state to take over Catholic schools during
certain hours when only secular instruction would be given
by teachers who would ordinarily teach in the Catholic
schools. Specifically Catholic instruction would then
be reserved for after hours.[46]

---

[45]Quoted in Barry, p. 119.

[46]The text of Ireland's speech is included in an
appendix in Daniel F. Reilly, The School Controversy,
1891-1893 (New York: Arno Press, 1969).

For many in the church, Ireland had gone too far in his accommodation with the state. After years of struggle to create and support parochial schools, Catholics were disturbed by even the suggestion that the effort could be abandoned. Even limited praise of public education seemed to undermine the primary argument used to justify the existence of Catholic schools--the fundamental inadequacy of education removed from the influence of religion. Criticism of Ireland intensified when he actually implemented his second proposal by turning over the parochial schools in Faribault and Stillwater, Minnesota to the local school board. Ireland's views received theoretical support from Thomas Bouquillon's publication in 1891 of Education: To Whom Does It Belong? Dr. Bouquillon, a professor at Catholic University, argued, contrary to conservative opinion, that the state had rights with regard to education independent of any specifically granted through the church.

Conservatives in the church felt Ireland and Bouquillon were in direct conflict with the decrees of the Councils of Baltimore on parochial schools and petitioned Rome to begin a formal investigation of the orthodoxy of Ireland's educational arrangement. Pope Leo XIII responded in 1892

> that the arrangement entered into by
> Archbishop Ireland concerning the schools
> at Faribault and Stillwater, taking into
> consideration all the circumstances, can
> be tolerated.[47]

---

[47]Ibid., p. 162.

It should be noted that Ireland's experiment was standard practice at the time in many European countries and in the United States, the conservative Bishop McQuaid had entered into a similar arrangement in his diocese of Rochester.

However, Leo's judgment failed to resolve the controversy. Liberals and conservatives each interpreted the Pope's "toleration" of Ireland's plan as a vindication of their own positions. To settle the matter, Leo sent Cardinal Satolli to make a first hand inspection of the situation. After his investigation, Satolli presented fourteen propositions for acceptance by the U.S. bishops that seemed to support the liberal position on the schools.

Not to be defeated and convinced that the Pope failed to appreciate the significance of Ireland's views in the context of the U.S. church, conservatives again appealed to Rome. In a conciliatory, but firm stance, the Pope upheld Satolli's resolution while reaffirming the educational legislation of the Councils. Since Satolli's propositions challenged several key features of the 1884 Council legislation, including the right of bishops to refuse absolution to parents who failed to send their children to Catholic schools and the legitimacy of children receiving strictly secular instruction from state schools, the Pope, while asserting his authority over the affairs of the church in America, avoided setting definitive standards for U.S. educational policy.

Ethos and Education at the Turn of the Century

Though Rome acted tentatively in the handling of the educational controversy at the end of the nineteenth century,
the tide soon turned decisively against the liberal cause.
In 1899 Leo XIII issued an Apostolic Letter addressed to the
church in America condemning "Americanism." This encyclical,
Testem Benevolentiae, represented "the implicit repudiation of
the liberals' attempt to make the American values of self-ini-
tiative, democracy, and freedom a model for the Church."[48] A
papal condemnation of Modernism in 1907 reinforced the forces
of conservatism, authoritarianism, and ultramontanism in the
U.S. by restricting certain lines of theological investigation
in scriptural and apologetic studies, effectively placing a halt
to an intellectual movement in U.S. Catholic seminaries in the
first decade of the twentieth century.

Between 1899 and 1917 during what has been called "an age
of transition" for the U.S. Catholic Church, new immigration
from southern and eastern Europe continued to reinforce the
church's "foreign" image among native Protestants and to
fuel ethnic diviseness within the church. Conflicts over
the cultural ethos of Catholicism helped ethnic parishes,
schools, and social organizations to flourish. At the same
time, the assimilation process continued among older ethnic
groups with Catholics beginning to establish themselves in
business and politics. However, gradual Americanization took

---

[48]Curran, pp. 497-98.

place with little leadership or direction from the Catholic
hierarchy in the areas of political and social life, although
some few Catholics were involved in social reform movements
in the progressive era.

Rome paid heed to the growing size, maturity and stability
of the Catholic Church in the U.S. in 1908 by eliminating the
church's mission status and removing it from under the jurisdiction of the Congregation for Propagation of the Faith.
Despite this improved status, the U.S. church lacked both
unity and leadership in this "era of confused silence and
inaction." While the actions of Rome at the turn of the
century were decisive in stifling the spirit of accommodation, innovation and adaptation that had characterized the
Americanizers' cause, there is evidence to suggest that, both
culturally and educationally, the liberal spirit was not completely submerged. In other words, as the church entered its
"ghetto period" after World War I, "the major problem of the
Americanist controversy--the manner of the adaptation of
Catholicism to the American scene--remained unresolved."[49]

---

[49]Thomas T. McAvoy, "The Catholic Minority after the
Americanist Controversy, 1899-1917: A Survey," Review of
Politics 21 (1959):55.

Chapter II

THE 1920'S: "CATHOLICISM UNBOUND" AND UNDER SIEGE

World War I marked a turning point in the self-consciousness of the Catholic community in the United States. Catholics
referred to their "return from exile"[1] when their active
support for the war won national approbation and new public
respect for the church in the U.S. The end of large scale
immigration in the 1920's stabilized the growth of U.S.
Catholicism, and for the first time, Catholics as a group
began making steady social and economic advances. A distinctively American Catholic identity was emerging for
the "immigrant church" as war hastened the assimilation
of recently arrived immigrants and inspired a growing sense
of solidarity among the church's ethnic constituencies.
A new spirit of confidence and "having arrived" among U.S.
Catholics accounts for James Hennesey's characterization
of the church in the 1920's as "Catholicism Unbound."[2]

Surveying their accomplishments in 1920, Catholic
church leaders took immense pride in the growth and
development of the Catholic school system. With meager

---

[1]William M. Halsey, The Survival of American Innocence:
Catholicism in an Era of Disillusionment, 1920-1940 (Notre
Dame, Indiana: University of Notre Dame Press, 1980), p. 8.

[2]American Catholics: A History of the Roman Catholic
Community in the United States (New York: Oxford University
Press, 1981), p. 234.

resources but much determination Catholics had created
an educational enterprise without parallel in the church's
history whose vast size and scope was a tribute to the
loyalty of American Catholics to their church. By 1920,
6,551 parish schools were operating in the United States
with enrollments reaching nearly one million eight hundred
thousand students. Secondary education was on a much smaller
scale, but growing with one hundred thirty thousand students
attending 1,552 Catholic high schools.[3]

In addition, major steps had been taken to insure
the quality and to improve the coordination of the work
of the schools. Catholic University of America, founded
in 1886 as an intellectual center of American Catholic life,
offered national education leadership beginning in the
early 1900's, especially through the work of its department
of education. Among its contributions were the training
of the first generation of priests to serve as diocesan
superintendents of Catholic schools, the establishment of
Catholic Sisters College for the professional education of
women religious teachers, the development of a program of
affiliation to upgrade the standards of Catholic high
schools, the creation of Catholic religion and reading
textbooks for use in the schools, and the publication

---

[3]Directory of Catholic Colleges and Schools 1932-
1933 (Washington, D.C.: National Catholic Welfare Conference,
1932), pp. 100, 194.

of the first Catholic professional education journal, The
Catholic Education Review. [4]

Other professional and popular journals serving the
needs and interests of Catholic teachers had begun circula-
tion in the early 1900's including The Catholic School
Journal, Catholic School Interests, The North American
Teacher, and The Sower, an English journal of Catholic education. While some of these periodicals offered articles
on educational theory and principles, others served primarily
as a practical resource for teaching methods, course out-
lines, lessons, projects, games and other activities for
actual classroom use. [5]

Two agencies in particular contributed to the increasing unity and systematization of Catholic schooling in
America. The Catholic Educational Association founded in
1904 (in 1928 "National" was added to the title) grew out
of the conviction that Catholic education at the turn of
the century was "being done by independent and individual

---

[4] John F. Murphy describes the important role played
by Thomas Edward Shields in these developments at Catholic
University in "Thomas Edward Shields: Religious Educator"
(Ph.D. dissertation, Columbia University, 1971). Another
account of the University's educational leadership is offered
by Rita Watrin in The Founding and Development of the Program
of Affiliation of The Catholic University of America: 1912
to 1939 (Washington, D.C.: Catholic University of America
Press, 1966), pp. 1-120.

[5] James E. Cummings, "Service Journals for Catholic
Educators," National Catholic Welfare Council Bulletin 11
(August 1929):14-15 (hereafter cited as NCWC Bulletin).

units, without that cohesiveness which comes from the unity
of purpose and the harmony of parts," and thus a need for
some organization which would bring U.S. Catholic educators
together "to discuss the means and methods by which the
best results in education may be attained."[6] Although voluntary in nature, the CEA provided a forum for the discussion of common educational problems and concerns and soon
became instrumental in setting the tone and direction of
Catholic educational policy and practice across the country.[7]
While the focus of the CEA was primarily to build up the
internal resources of the schools, the task of representing Catholic school interests to the larger public fell
more directly to the National Catholic Welfare Council. The
American Catholic hierarchy established the NCWC department
of education in 1919 to serve as a clearinghouse for information concerning Catholic educational activities and to present the church's official position on matters concerning
educational policy and practice.[8]

---

[6]Thomas J. Conaty, rector of Catholic University,
speaking at the Conference of Catholic Seminaries in 1898.
Cited by Edgar Patrick McCarren, "The Origins and Early Years
of the National Catholic Educational Association" (Ph.D.
dissertation, Catholic University of America, 1966), p. 128.

[7]See Constance Welch, "The National Catholic Educational
Association: Its Contribution to American Education: A
Synthesis" (Ph.D. dissertation, Stanford University, 1947).

[8]"Hierarchy Approves Work of Welfare Council," NCWC
Bulletin 2 (October 1920):6-8. See also James E. Cummings,
"Catholic Education and the National Catholic Welfare Conference"
in Vital Problems of Catholic Education in the United States,
ed. Roy J. Deferrari (Washington, D.C.: Catholic University
of America Press, 1939), pp. 50-58.

Another significant development underway by 1920 was
the organization of the schools along diocesan lines. In
the nineteenth century competition rather than cooperation
in general characterized the relations among Catholic
schools. Intense ethnic rivalries and the desires of pastors
and religious superiors to preserve their autonomy in the
operation of parochial and private Catholic schools were
in large part responsible for the highly decentralized structure of Catholic education.[9] But by the turn of the century,
problems resulting from the rapid growth in the number of
schools and increasing enrollments created a need for more
adequate supervision and administration of the schools. To
meet this need, bishops had begun establishing diocesan
school boards in the 1890's. By 1920, in an effort to
tighten administrative control and improve efficiency, the
diocesan school board was being systematically replaced by
a single diocesan superintendent of schools directly responsible
to the bishop, whose tasks included the supervision of instruction, inspection of facilities, selection of textbooks
and uniform courses of study, establishment of teacher
certification requirements, and educational research and
testing.[10]

---

[9]Sanders, p. 45.

[10]See John M. Voelker, "The Diocesan Superintendent of
Schools: A Study of the Historical Development and Functional
Status of His Office" (Ph.D. dissertation, Catholic University
of America, 1935) and William G. Scanlon, "The Development of
the American Catholic Diocesan Board of Education, 1884-1966"
(Ed.D. dissertation, New York University, 1967).

Catholic educators viewed these developments with
pride and optimism, satisfied that every effort was being
made to fulfill the vision of a complete system of Catholic
education in the U.S. The reports of the 1919 Catholic
Educational Association meeting expressed the prevalent
mood:

> Catholic education in this country was never
> in a more flourishing condition. Our schools
> cannot accommodate all those who desire admission.
> For years past there have been no public contro-
> versies among Catholics on educational policies
> and problems; harmony, good will, and unity have
> characterized the relations of Catholic educators,
> and there have been cooperation and progress in
> all lines of the work.
> Catholic education in the United States now has
> a solid support of Catholic opinion behind it and
> parents are eager that their children should have
> a Christian education. Catholic education will
> now hold its own in comparison with any education
> given in the country.[11]

In spite of the fact that the schools were as yet reaching
barely half of school-age Catholic youth, educational leaders
felt that the major battle--convincing Catholic parents of
the need for Catholic schools--had been essentially won.
And despite serious obstacles--lack of money and the need
for more school buildings and teaching staffs--the Catholic
educational community shared the expectations of the
Rt. Rev. Mgr. Philip R. McDevitt who in 1910 predicted that

> we may look forward hopefully and confidently
> to the time as not far distant when every

[11]"Introduction," The Catholic Educational Association
Bulletin 16 (November 1919):7 (hereafter cited as CEA Bulletin).

Catholic child in the U.S. may enjoy his true
inheritance--a Catholic education.[12]

Catholic Schools Under Siege

However, only four years later, McDevitt was to have

a much more pessimistic assessment of the future of Catholic

schools.

> Signs are not wanting which indicate a
> tendency on the part of the State, not
> indeed to destroy liberty of teaching,
> but to modify the civil authority's pas-
> sive or indifferent attitude towards pri-
> vate schools, to extend its jurisdiction
> in matters educational, and to bring it
> to bear more fully upon private schools
> and take away some of the so-called privi-
> leges these schools enjoy . . . . The
> tendency to increase the authority of the
> State in education and to restrict or to
> weaken the freedom which private schools
> have always enjoyed, is one of the impor-
> tant and significant facts which Catholics
> must notice in the consideration of the pre-
> sent status of Catholic schools.[13]

Indeed, storm clouds were brewing on what had seemed a clear

and bright horizon for Catholic schools. The nature, purpose,

methods, and organization of public schooling in the United

States were undergoing major shifts under the impact of

progressive educational reform. Meanwhile the cultural

---

[12]McDevitt, superintendent of Catholic schools in
Philadelphia, is quoted in James A. Burns, The Growth and
Development of the Catholic School System in the United
States (New York: Benziger Bros., 1912; reprint ed., New
York: Arno Press & The New York Times, 1969), p. 359.

[13]Cited by John A. Nepper, "School Legislation in
Nebraska," CEA Bulletin 16 (November 1919):268.

ferment generated during World War I and its aftermath--
nationalistic fervor, fear of immigrants, concerns over
Americanism, and the revival of anti-Catholic hostilities--
produced a crusade for conformity that placed Roman
Catholicism squarely on the defensive in the "tribal twenties."
Critics began casting suspicion on the legitimacy and effectiveness of Catholic schools in American society. Pressures
on the schools mounted as state and federal legislative
measures threatened the independence and even more seriously,
the very existence of Catholic schooling in the U.S.

The Reform of Public Education

In 1920 public schools in the United States were in
the midst of a major transformation as a result of the multi-
leveled movement known as progressive education. Historically Americans had always placed faith in the power of
education to create the good society. Their commitments
to public schooling were built on "the sense of an inex-
tricable relationship between education and national
progress." Thus in the 1890's, with Americans acutely
troubled by the social effects of rapid industrialization,
immigration and urbanization, Joseph Mayer Rice published
a series of articles describing the terrible conditions
he had observed in America's public schools in The Forum
and touched off "a nationwide torrent of criticism, innovation,

and reform that soon took on all the earmarks of a social movement."[14]

Analysts of progressive education identify three distinctive but often interwoven aspects of the reform movement that had significant impact on public schooling in the 1920's. Inspired by the claims of the emerging social and psychological sciences, educators began to conceive of the public schools as an instrument for social reform. In addition to teaching basic skills, the public increasingly demanded that schools offer vocational training, facilitate personal growth and social adjustment, and Americanize foreign-born immigrants and their children. Child-centered or pedagogical progressives sought to develop a new approach to teaching and learning in the schools. The uniform curriculum and traditional recitation methods were being replaced by differentiated curriculums and activity methods geared to the abilities, needs and interests of the child. A third group, "administrative progressives,"[15] impressed with the success of business and industry, were convinced that science held the key to improving the social efficiency

[14]Lawrence A. Cremin, The Transformation of the School: Progressivism in American Education 1876-1957 (New York: Random House, Vintage Books, 1964), pp. 8, 22.

[15]This term is used by David B. Tyack, The One Best System: A History of American Urban Education (Cambridge, Massachusetts and London, England: Harvard University Press, 1974), pp. 182-98.

of the schools. Through professional training of school personnel, adoption of bureaucratic organizational structures,
and the use of scientific measures of student ability, they
introduced "the cult of efficiency"[16] into the administration and organization of U.S. public schools.

This third group in particular turned to the state
to further their program for the standardization and professionalization of public schooling. By 1920 all but six
states had established state boards of education to enforce
uniform standards for the certification of teachers, principals and superintendents, the development of curriculum,
and the organization and administration of the schools. Efforts to expand the role of the federal government in education resulted in a series of bills introduced before Congress
in the twenties, beginning with the Smith-Towner Bill in
1919, to create a federal department of education, establish a cabinet-level post of secretary of education, and
provide federal funds to the states for education. Catholics
feared such measures would eventually result in excessive
government interference in Catholic schools in addition
to giving public schools a decisive financial advantage
over Catholic schools, especially in view of the emphasis
on education as a means of social control after World War I.[17]

---

[16]Raymond E. Callahan, Education and the Cult of
Efficiency: A Study of the Social Forces that have Shaped
the Administration of the Public Schools (Chicago: University of Chicago Press, 1962).

[17]"Educational Legislation," School and Society 9 (29
March 1919):391-92. See also "Welfare Council Issues Statement
on the Smith-Towner Bill," NCWC Bulletin 2 (March-April 1920):24.

The War and "Americanization"

Over nine million immigrants from southern and eastern
Europe had streamed into the United States between 1880 and
1914 and settled in congested urban centers in the northeast
and middle west. Coming from countries considered the most
politically, socially and economically backwards of Europe,
this "new immigration" generated intense antipathy from
Americans disturbed by the poverty, squalor and crime endemic
to urban slums.

The outbreak of war in Europe in 1914 aroused anxious
concern among many citizens about the effect of massive
numbers of "unassimilated" foreigners--many of them illiterate
and unable to speak English--on national unity and strength.
Conscious of the threat of divided loyalties among "hyphen-
ated Americans" who might be called to support a war against
their former homelands, Americans began to lose their
historic confidence in the assimilative powers of American
institutions, particularly the schools, and, according to
John Higham, "a conscious drive to hasten the assimilative
process, to heat and stir the melting pot emerged."[18]

"Americanization" became a popular crusade with the
proclamation of July 4, 1915 as "Americanization Day."
Schools, churches, businesses and industry, as well as

_____

[18]Higham, p. 235. See also Edward Hartmann, The
Movement to Americanize the Immigrant (New York: Columbia
University, 1948).

state and federal governmental agencies became involved
in an intensive education campaign to teach newly arrived
immigrants English, to encourage their abandonment of
foreign cultural manners and adaptation to American ways,
and to promote patriotism and national loyalty among the
entire populace.

Xenophobic fears spread with America's entrance into
the war and furthered support for the militantly nationalistic programs and goals of "100 per cent Americanizers."
Their demands for total conformity and fervent expressions
of national loyalty led to tragic restrictions on German
American citizens and the suppression of German culture.

> By threat and rhetoric, 100 per cent American-
> izers opened a frontal assault on foreign in-
> fluence in American life. They set about to
> stampede immigrants into citizenship, into
> adoption of the English language, and into an
> unquestioning reverence for existing American
> institutions. They bade them abandon entirely
> their Old World loyalties, customs, and memories.
> They used high-pressure, steamroller tactics.
> They cajoled and they commanded.[19]

They also used the political process to enact educational
legislation to enforce their ideological campaign. "Americanizers" had raised an alarm across the nation about the
dangers of a multi-lingual society and by 1919 fifteen
states had passed laws requiring the exclusive use of the
English language in all primary schools, both public and
private.[20] By 1923, thirty-four states had enacted similar

---

[19]Higham, p. 247.

[20]Ibid., p. 260.

legislation.[21] Such laws had serious consequences for a
Catholic school system organized essentially upon ethnic
lines where new immigrants were often taught in their
native tongue. In addition, xenophobic fears were also
responsible for legislation requiring loyalty oaths of
all public and private school teachers, the teaching of
courses in American history, civics, and patriotism in private and public schools,[22] and citizenship as a pre-requi-
site for obtaining teaching certification.[23]

The wave of strikes and radical dissent that swept
the country during the Big Red Scare fueled demands for
social conformity. Nativists linked radicalism to foreign-
born immigrants and rededicated themselves to the task of
"Americanization" as an "antidote to Bolshevism." But by
1920 nativists were giving up faith in the assimilative
capacity of the immigrant and instead turned their efforts to
enacting immigration restriction legislation.

---

[21]Arnold H. Leibowitz, "Language as a Means of Social
Control: The United States Experience," paper delivered at
the VIII World Congress of Sociology, Toronto, Canada (Bethesda,
Maryland: ERIC Document Reproduction Service, ED093168, 1974),
p. 14.

[22]C. N. Lischka in Private Schools and State Laws reported
that by 1926, six states had laws requiring loyalty oaths and
over half the states mandated citizenship courses. Cited by
James T. O'Dowd, Standardization and Its Influence on Catholic
Secondary Education in the United States (Washington, D.C.:
Catholic Education Press, 1936), p. 5.

[23]C. N. Lischka, "State Laws Affecting Parochial
Schools," NCWC Bulletin 3 (June 1921):21.

Though it collapsed as a popular movement in 1920,
the assumptions and goals of "Americanization" had become
firmly entrenched in the public's expectations of schooling in American society. The war had impressed upon the
American people the need for national unity and purpose
at a time when traditional social bonds all seemed threatened.
This situation intensified Americans' commitment to the public
schools as "the one best system" for the maintenance and
transmission of a common culture and national identity.
These schools could be made accountable to serve the nation's
interests, but what was to be done if large numbers of
citizens, especially those who because of class, religion
or ethnicity were already set apart from the cultural and
social mainstream, continued to be educated outside of
state controlled institutions? The problems of social
fragmentation highlighted by the war raised growing public
concern about the goals, purposes and outcomes of non-
public education that resulted in increasing demands for
public scrutiny of institutions claiming to function as
a substitute for public schools.

Nativist Attacks on Catholic Schools

Public concerns over parochial schools were intensified by the re-emergence of aggressive anti-Catholic nativism
in the 1920's, particularly among rural Protestant funda-
mentalists alarmed by the expansion of urban-based Catholicism at a time when their own position of influence in

American social and political life was significantly erod-
ing. Built upon the intense nationalistic fervor and suspicion of foreign influence in American life generated
by World War I, nativist fears were fueled by an economic
depression, massive increases in immigration from Catholic
countries after the war, and, most directly, Catholic resistance to Prohibition.[26] Anti-Catholic organizations
such as the Klu Klux Klan, the Patriotic Knights of American
Liberty, the Defenders of Truth Society, the Protestant Guard,
and the Fellowship Forum all flourished in the 1920's and
revived historic fears of a papal plot to subvert American
institutions and ideals.

Anti-Catholic literature during this period continued
to stress the fundamental incompatibility of "Romanism"
and "Americanism." Alien Rome, for example, affirmed
Theodore Roosevelt's statement that "the Catholic Church
is in no way suited to this country . . . for its thought is
Latin and entirely at variance with the democratic thought
of our country and institutions." The tract charged that
"Romanism" stood for autocracy and was "opposed to freedom
of speech, freedom of the press, freedom of religion and
the free public school for all the Nation's children."
It further claimed the existence of a vast, sinister effort
by the U.S. Catholic hierarchy to "Romanize" the United
States through immigration.

---

[26]Higham, pp. 286-99.

> Political Romanism has succeeded through the
> large influx of foreign elements in capturing
> the control of entire states, and is moving
> aggressively ahead . . . for national conquest
> . . . . Its political busyings here are rankly
> subversive of American democracy and American
> free institutions.

Once arrived in this country immigrant children were isolated

in parochial schools as "a barrier to true Americanization"

while Catholic teachers and administrators infiltrated

the public school system to subvert America from within.

> Our educational ideals are fundamentally Protes-
> tant. The first colonists came to America that
> they might be separated by the width of the
> Atlantic from the reactionary, tyrannical ideas
> of Rome. It is the undermining of our Protestant
> educational system by the foreign masses from
> Eastern and Southern Europe that now threatens
> the failure of our American democracy.[27]

Attacks on the Catholic school system were an intrinsic

part of the nativist campaign. One magazine referred to

parochial schools as

> a destroyer of American Patriotism, discredit-
> ing and boycotting the American Public School--
> the hope and foundation of American Democracy.[28]

Franklin Ford, editor of The American Standard, cited statis-

tics to show that the

> Romanist minority, trained by nuns and priests
> in the technique of mental reservations, false
> oaths, cancellation of misdeeds through the
> confessional, etc., furnish the majority of our
> criminals.

---

[27]Bertrand M. Tipple, Alien Rome (Washington, D.C.:
Protestant Guards, 1924), pp. 1, 3, 35.

[28]Quoted from the editorial policy statement of
The Crusader, ed. D. J. Gordon, n.d.

He also charged the schools with disseminating "un-American political doctrine" by their refusal to recognize "the supreme jurisdiction of the State" in education. One illustration showed a black-robed priest pushing children into a parochial school draped with banners proclaiming "superstition," "poverty" and "illiteracy;" while he blocked the entrance to the public school whose banners read "liberty," "Democracy" and "intelligence."[29]

Thomas Watson, founder of Watson's Magazine and populist candidate for the presidency in 1904, took up in detail nativists' objections to Catholic schools and warned of the dire consequences of Catholic-educated children for the future of democracy.

> The Catholics denounce secular education and public schools--Why?
> Because, under the papal system, the child is never to be permitted to do its own thinking.
> Its plastic brain must be papalized, in order that the child--grown to manhood or womanhood-- will be atrophied on one side of its mind.
> In other words, Catholic education seeks to prevent the boy and girl from knowing any truth which may set in motion those dynamic spurs of progress, namely, doubt, desire to see the other side, determination to investigate and form INDEPENDENT OPINIONS.
> Educate youth in this Catholic way, and the consequences are logical: the children graduate in obedience; feel no divine thirst for knowledge; cringe to the priest; look to him for guidance and control; lose mental self-reliance, and gradually cease to be liberals, progressives, democrats,

---

[29]"Moral (?) Benefits of R.C. Parochial Training," and "Right to Manage and Teach in Our Schools Demanded by Their Roman Catholic Enemies," The American Standard, 1 September 1930, p. 9.

republicans--<u>believers</u> <u>in</u> <u>the</u> <u>capacity</u> <u>of</u> <u>the</u>
<u>people</u> <u>to</u> <u>govern</u> <u>themselves</u>.
A Catholic, imbued with the idea that he is
not entitled to any voice in church affairs, and
contented with the dependent position of the man
who must silently pay and obey, <u>soon</u> <u>accepts</u> <u>the</u>
POLITICAL <u>doctrine</u> <u>of</u> <u>his</u> <u>church</u>, also; and he
comes to believe that he has no right to choose
rulers, make laws, think for himself on public
questions, or to take any initiative, whatever.
Priest Ridden in Church, he is ready to Become
Priest-Ridden in State.[30]

Though the inflammatory rhetoric of the nativist press
was reason enough for grave concern among Catholics, even
more disturbing was the support of anti-Catholic organizations
for restrictive measures against Roman Catholics and their
institutions. Many nativist groups worked vigorously to
oppose state aid for parochial schools, to secure state
inspection of Catholic hospitals, orphanages, convents and
schools, to exact compulsory public school attendance laws,
to establish a federal department of education, and to
eliminate Catholic teachers and supervisors from public
schools.

"A National Conspiracy": The Cases
of Nebraska and Oregon

In the early 1920's Catholics became convinced that
they were facing what one editorial described as a "national
Conspiracy Against the Catholic Schools."

---

[30]<u>Roman Catholics in America falsifying history and</u>
<u>poisoning the minds of Protestant School-children</u> (Thompson,
Georgia: Press of the Jefferson Publishing Co., 1917), p. 5.

> Very powerful organizations are making hostility
> towards religious education a major plank in
> their programs. They are likewise uniting so
> as to realize more efficaciously and quickly
> their plans. There is no longer any secrecy
> about this opposition.[31]

Though willing and eager to demonstrate their conscientious
regard for their educational and civic responsibilities,
Catholic leaders were extremely sensitive to the anti-Catholic
sentiment supporting educational reform legislation and wary
of the potentially devastating effects of government intervention on their schools. Their worst fears were given
substance by developing educational legislation in two states
in particular: Nebraska and Oregon.

In 1917, a survey conducted by the Women's Committee
of the Council of Defense of the state of Nebraska confirmed
the extensive and often exclusive use of German in Lutheran
and Catholic parochial schools throughout the state. Attendance at these schools in many counties had forced public
schools to close for lack of students. One Catholic ob-
server described the impact of these revelations on an
aroused public.

> A wave of bigotry . . . swept over the State
> . . . . Under the bright sun of patriotism
> were drawn up the dangerous clouds of hyper-
> nationalism which like a cyclone swooped down
> upon us, affecting men with a reform-hysteria
> that soon manifested symptoms of persecution.[32]

---

[31] NCWC Bulletin 4 (October 1922):21.

[32] Nepper, p. 269. For discussions of Nebraska's educational legislation, see also Paul L. Blakely, S.J., "The
Trend of Educational Legislation," CEA Bulletin 16 (November
1919):450-75 and G. W. A. Luckey, "Important Changes in the
Nebraska School Law," Educational Review 58 (September 1919):
109-19.

Responding to public pressure, the state legislature in
1919 enacted laws to prohibit instruction in any language
other than English in all private and public schools in
the elementary grades, to require that all teachers in
private and public schools be full citizens, and to prohibit
religious teachers in state schools (the "Religious Garb
Bill"). In addition, a bill to require all children between the ages of seven and fifteen to attend public schools
was defeated by a single vote. A substitute measure to
impose strict regulation of all private schools was proposed.
In its original form, the "Burney Bill" would have given
public officials virtually complete authority over the conduct of private schools. As one critic noted wryly, this
"Draconian law would make public schools out of our private
schools in every thing save the liberty of paying the bills."[33]

As a result largely of Catholic lobbying efforts,
a compromise measure was finally adopted that set less
comprehensive standards for the conduct of private schools.
The new law subjected all private schools to "the general
school laws of the State" applying "to grades, qualification and certification of teachers and promotion of pupils."
Courses of study were to be "substantially the same as
those given in the public schools," including required
courses in American history and government and the conduct
of patriotic exercises prescribed by the State superintendent

[33]Nepper, p. 273.

of education. Teachers in any school, public or private, would be required to obtain state teaching certificates. The bill also established the right of public school officials to inspect private schools and to

> report to the proper officials any evidence of the use of any text-books or of any activities, instruction or propaganda therein subversive of American institutions and republican form of government or good citizenship or of failure to observe any of the provisions of this act.

A major concession won by Catholic opponents was a clause denying any intent "to interfere with religious instruction" and affirming the right of private schools "to select and purchase text-books, equipment and supplies, to employ teachers and to have and exercise the general management of the school."[34]

The attempt to restrict attendance at non-public schools was more successful in the state of Oregon. Fear of immigrants, concerns over "Americanism" and anti-Catholicism were also motivations behind a 1922 initiative in Oregon to make public schooling compulsory for all children between the ages of eight and sixteen.[35] Supporters of the Oregon bill, including the Klu Klux Klan and the Oregon Scottish Rite

---

[34]The text of the bill is cited in full by Nepper, pp. 273-74.

[35]See David B. Tyack, "The Perils of Pluralism: The Background of the Pierce Case," American Historical Review 74 (October 1968):74-98; and Lloyd P. Jorgenson, "The Oregon School Law of 1922: Passage and Sequel," Catholic Historical Review 54 (October 1968):455-66. The text of the law and a complete record of the legal proceedings are provided in Oregon School Cases: Complete Record (Baltimore: Westminster Press, 1925).

Masons, tried to define the issue as a battle between those
who believed in "Free Public Schools" as "the cornerstone
of good government" and "enemies of the Republic" who
were "seeking to destroy it." Vicious campaign propaganda
asserted that "vast masses of our population . . . have no
more pedigree than the street dogs and cats"; and Klansman
Fred Gifford, a chief sponsor of the school bill warned
Oregonians that "somehow these mongrel hordes must be Americanized."[36] Catholics were urged to "abolish the parochial
grade school" where students would "master Histomorphology,
the Petrine Supremacy, Transubstantiation and trace the
original authority and ecclesiastical record of Peter's
Pence," and "join with other Americans in building up the
Public School."[37]

Many Americans had looked with disfavor on Catholic
schools throughout the nineteenth century, but the autonomy
and legal right of such schools to exist had never been in
such serious jeopardy. Compulsory public school attendance
laws had been narrowly defeated in state referendums in
Michigan twice, and a dozen more states were considering

---

[36]Quoted in Tyack, pp. 79-80.

[37]Lem Dever, a leading Klan publicist and George Estes,
author of The Roman Katholic Kingdom and The Ku Klux Klan,
cited by Tyack, pp. 80-81. Tyack notes the irony of these
appeals in a state such as Oregon. "In 1920 the state had
only 13 per cent foreign-born inhabitants (one half of them
naturalized), only 0.3 per cent Negroes, only about 8 per
cent Catholics. Almost 95 per cent of all children between
seven and thirteen were in school; over 93 per cent of these
students attended public schools." p. 76.

similar restrictions against private schools if the Oregon measure were to prove successful. Though the U.S. Supreme Court was to reject in 1923 Nebraska's prohibition against the use of foreign languages in schools and Oregon's compulsory public school attendance law in 1925, these and similar challenges to the integrity and independence of Catholic schools weighed heavily on Catholic school supporters and caused a major shift in the concerns and focus of educational leaders in the early 1920's.

Educational Issues in the 1920's

Until the turn of the century, church leaders had been primarily concerned with two educational tasks: building up and coordinating an expanding school system and convincing Catholics of the need for separate schools for religious education. With success on both of these fronts relatively secure by 1920, church leaders faced a different set of challenges from the gradual decline in ethnicity within the church and external pressures threatening the schools' survival.

The social changes in the Catholic population created what Philip Gleason describes as a "crisis of Americanization" for the church as an institution. The problem as Gleason defines it is that

> changes in the social composition and outlook
> of the group require a reshaping of Catholic

institutions to bring them into line with the
shifting configuration of the clientele whose
needs they serve and whose values they symbolize
and embody.[38]

Yet the church was officially committed to an ideological

position that overtly and explicitly discouraged the kind

of intellectual and cultural creativity that could have

guided institutional reform. Catholic schools in particu-

lar were caught in this tension between the impulses toward

transformation and conservation. In order to hold Catholic

students, the schools needed to appeal to the desires and

expectations of an upwardly mobile and increasingly assimi-

lated population. On the other hand its primary goal was

to communicate a "Catholic" ethos and worldview contrary

to many accepted social and cultural norms.

Moreover, with the survival of Catholic schools at

stake, this task became even more complicated as church

leaders struggled to present a rationale for Catholic

schools that would allay fears and ward off the threat of

hostile legislation while preserving the institutional

autonomy and the essential integrity of a Catholic vision

of education. To calm public fears church leaders wanted

to avoid controversial or antagonistic positions. However,

they would not make any accommodations that would seriously

jeopardize the church's control over its own educational

enterprise.

---

[38]"The Crisis of Americanization" in Catholicism in
America (New York: Harper & Row, 1970), pp. 149-50.

The dilemma facing Catholic educators on a national level by 1920 was perhaps best described by Howard Weisz:

> Advocates of . . . parochial schools were faced with the difficulty of arguing both that the schools were American and that they were very different from all other American schools. If parochial schools were not demonstrably American they could not survive pressure from their enemies, and if they were not different, then they had no reason to exist.[39]

Though church leaders in the 1920's were convinced of the need for a strong and united front in defending the schools, they wrestled among themselves with questions of the distinctiveness as well as the complementarity between American and Catholic traditions, especially with regard to four major educational issues: 1) a rationale for Catholic educational separatism, 2) the schools' social and civic responsibilities, 3) the authority of church and state in the control and supervision of Catholic schools, and 4) the determination of educational standards in the conduct of Catholic schools.

In coming to terms with these issues in the 1920's, the church's educational policies and practices reflected the attempt to walk a "tightrope between a too foreign looking resistance to accommodation and a too easy affirmation of American mores."[40] Though the defensive, isolationist fears of nineteenth century conservative Catholicism

---

[39]"Irish-American Attitudes," p. 158.

[40]David J. O'Brien, "Some Reflections on the Catholic Experience in the United States," The Catholic Church: The United States Experience, ed. Irene Woodward, S.N.J.M. (New York: Paulist Press, 1979), p. 9.

were still evident in the twentieth, Catholic schooling,
subtly influenced by the social forces of modernization,
bureaucratization, and professionalization, took on a distinctively "American" cast.

Chapter III

CATHOLIC SCHOOLS IN AMERICAN SOCIETY

In their campaign against parochial schools, nativists
in the 1920's frequently charged that "Romanism" was fundamentally incompatible with American values and ideals.
Ironically, until the turn of the century, that was pre-
cisely the view that motivated conservative Catholic pre-
lates to urge support for a separate Catholic school system.
Convinced that Americanization threatened the immigrant's
faith, conservatives saw Catholic schools as a means to
insure immigrants' loyalty to the church by enabling them
to retain the language and customs of their former homeland.

However, while a negative assessment of American culture was crucial in founding Catholic schools, it was a
clear liability in the task of convincing the American
people of the public benefits of denominational schools.
In the 1920's cultural isolation was becoming increasingly
both inappropriate and dangerous as a rationale for Catholic
schools. English language parochial schools patronized
primarily by the Irish had already become significantly
"Americanized."[1] Support for the U.S. against Germany in
World War I was but one indication of the advancing assimilation of German-American citizens. Although newly arrived

---

[1] See Weisz, "Irish-American Attitudes."

immigrants from southern and eastern Europe continued to establish national parishes and schools to ease their transition to life in the U.S., rampant hostility toward "hyphenated-Americans" made it increasingly difficult for Catholic leaders to openly advocate cultural pluralism as an educational ideal.

This situation forced educational leaders to re-consider the educational mission of Catholic schools in American society. Church leaders were convinced that hostility towards the schools resulted from lack of public awareness of the nature, purposes and values of Catholic schooling. In contrast with the predominantly defensive, isolationist tone of Catholic school advocates during the early years of school establishment, church leaders in the 1920's argued that educational separatism constituted as much a service to the country as to the church. While continuing to insist on the need for Catholic schools, church leaders emphasized the fundamentally American identity and character of the schools. This apologetic stance was succinctly expressed in the official parish school motto adopted by the CEA in 1918: "For God and Country."

This educational vision was rooted in a distinctive American Catholic ethos that crystallized in the decade after World War I. Largely as a result of participation in the war and the gradual assimilation of older ethnic groups, U.S. Catholics were increasingly secure in their identity as both Americans and Catholics, convinced that

"the lines of service to one and the other parallel, support and sustain one another."[2] As the supervisor of
parochial schools in Portland, Maine declared:

> In spite of all this spoken for the contrary,
> the truths of faith and the principles of
> American democracy work together admirably
> in directing the daily actions of the Catholic
> citizen. With comparative ease, and with
> a sense of conviction, he can render to
> Caesar the things that are Caesar's, and to
> God the things that are God's.[3]

Catholics arrived at this newfound confidence, however,
at a time when major social and cultural upheavals were trans-
forming the character of American life. The transition
from a rural to an urban-based society that had eroded
Protestant influence provided for Catholics new avenues
of influence and power. World War I had shattered much of
Protestantism's liberal faith in the promises of American
life just as Catholics were becoming "secure enough to claim
America." Catholics saw themselves living in a "disintegrat-
ing world" where the forces of intellectual modernism,
secularism and materialism were causing the country to
abandon the religious ideals and values, the intellectual
and moral certainties that constituted the essence of
American idealism.[4] Thomas J. Shahan, president general
of the Catholic Educational Association, voiced this
assessment of the times in 1919:

---

[2] Archbishop John Glennon of St. Louis, quoted in
"Around the Conference Table," NCWC Bulletin 5 (March 1924):4.

[3] Cited by Joseph V. S. M'Clancy, "What the Superintendents are Doing," CER 20 (December 1920):590.

[4] This theme is developed by Halsey, pp. 2-4.

> The moral flowering of materialism is about
> us on all sides in suicide, divorce, juvenile
> crime; in the decay of old-time courtesy and
> good manners and in an unabashed selfishness;
> in lack of principle and moral stamina, and in
> other unpleasing facts of public and private
> life . . . . Materialism is an intellectual
> error, a social plague, an economic menace, and
> a political abyss.[5]

In response to this cultural fragmentation, Catholics began
"to construct a world impervious to the disruptions of
modernity," determined to defend the structure of values,
beliefs, and behaviors characteristic of what Henry May
characterized as nineteenth century "American innocence":

> belief in a rational and orderly universe, faith
> in progress as the essential character of the
> American experience, and recognition of a sys-
> tem of absolute moral values inherent in the
> structure of reality.[6]

This view helped to unite and reconcile differences
between conservatives, primarily concerned with preserving
the purity of Catholic faith, and liberals, eager for the
church to assume a more active role in American life. Both
groups held firm to the belief that religious faith was
essential to society and that its absence would inevitably
lead to anarchy and social ruin. In their particular version of civil faith, Catholics viewed the United States as
fundamentally a Christian country, democracy as "essentially
a religious ideal,"[7] although Protestantism had proved an

---

[5]"First General Session," CEA Bulletin 16 (November 1919):52

[6]Cited by Halsey, p. 2.

[7]James H. Ryan, "Religious Education and Democracy,"
CER 21 (June 1923):324.

inadequate foundation. While disagreeing on the specific
implications of this vision of a Christian America, both
liberals and conservatives saw the mission of Catholicism
to "re-Americanize America"[8] by restoring the country to
its religious values and ideals. In historian Elizabeth
McKeown's words,

> the second decade of the century promised that
> Catholics by remaining loyal to traditions of
> the Church and by embracing the duties of Ameri-
> can citizenship, could provide the country with
> a spiritual center to ground its ideals and
> guarantee its progress.[9]

A Rationale for Catholic Schooling

Catholic leaders' understanding of the church's educational mission reflected the assumptions and the ambiguities
of this emerging Catholic consciousness. By maintaining the
unity of religion and education, Catholics viewed their
schools, in Shahan's words, as "the most vigorous protest
against this wasting disease of the modern mind"[10] and a
leaven for the transformation of the debased aspects of
American culture. In secularizing the public schools,
Catholics felt America had abandoned the original educational vision of the founders of the Republic. Thus

---

[8]Halsey, p. 3.

[9]"War and Welfare: A Study of American Catholic Leadership" (Ph.D. dissertation, University of Chicago, 1972), p. 33.

[10]Shahan, "Session," p. 52.

Catholic schools, even more than public schools were

> proving themselves the real bulwarks of our
> national life, the best conservers of our
> American ideals, the most effective training
> centers for secular education, and, more than
> all else, the fountain sources where our future
> American citizens receive the most thorough
> preparation for the fulfillment of their reli-
> gious and civic responsibilities.[11]

These twin social responsibilities--to Catholicize America

and to Americanize Catholics--became central to the church's

apologetic argument defending the unique qualities that made

educational separatism necessary and the public qualities

that made them socially desirable.

This two-sided mentality, at once defensive and apolo-

getic, is clearly revealed in the American hierarchy's

discussion of the church's educational mission in their

1919 pastoral letter to the U.S. church. Catholics were

required to maintain a "system of education distinct and

separate" primarily because of a positive vision of the

relation between religion and education. Understanding

education as ultimately a religious and moral enterprise,

the bishops insisted that education must

> accord the first place to religion, that is,
> to the knowledge of God and His law and must
> cultivate a spirit of obedience to His
> commands.

Ideally religious, moral, physical and intellectual capacities

should be developed harmoniously.

---

[11]"Our Catholic Schools," NCWC Bulletin 3 (June 1921):8.

> An education that quickens the intelligence and
> enriches the mind with knowledge, but fails to
> develop the will and direct it to the practice
> of virtue, may produce scholars, but it cannot
> produce good men.

The bishops rejected not only the elimination of explicit

religious instruction from formal schooling, but even more

fundamentally, any understanding of education that did not

account for the religious and moral dimensions of all knowledge.

> Religion should so permeate the knowledge
> disciplines that its influence will be felt
> in every circumstance of life, and be strength-
> ened as the mind advances to a fuller acquain-
> tance with nature and a riper experience with
> the realities of human existence.

The ability and commitment to provide this kind of wholistic

(or in its negative, exclusionary expression, totalistic)

education that would hold together religious education and

cultural transmission was what distinguished and identified

Catholic schooling.[12]

Joseph A. Dunney, diocesan superintendent of schools

in Albany, New York, in "The Parish School": Its Aims,

Procedures, and Problems amplified the implications of this

"permeation theory" of religious education in the conduct

of Catholic schools.

> Religion and education go together as one.
> They are twin travelers, these two inseparables
> on our road of life. They cannot, must not,
> be estranged, for they are interdependent,
> mutually helpful. The parish school sees
> to it that they go hand in hand; reason and
> faith, truth human and truth divine, facts
> of nature and facts of grace; supporting,
> explaining each other in a harmony that
> has its source in the mind of the Creator.
> Every element, every study is focused, its

---

[12]"Pastoral Letter of the Archbishops and Bishops of the
United States," Catholic Education in America: A Documentary
History, ed. Neil G. McCluskey, S.J. (New York: Teachers College,
Columbia University), pp. 186-88.

> light is made to mingle with the light of
> faith, and its relevancy with religion surely
> established . . . .
>   With this plan before her the Catholic
> teacher cannot afford to regard religion
> as a side study, a mere addition to the
> course . . . . We have to see that reli-
> gion is designedly woven into the warp and
> woof of the mind of both teacher and pupil.
> Its place is part and parcel of the emotional,
> and volitional activities. The ideas, facts,
> events, principles imparted should be so
> permeated with the thought of God that they
> will be operative in shaping the child for
> Christian activity, interest, occupation.
> Then the soul will be a dynamo, charged
> with the flash and fire of religious impulse,
> vital with a driving power of will, energiz-
> ing with that courage of heart which results
> in Christian conduct and responds daily to
> the divine power of grace that makes for
> righteousness.[13]

While insisting that separate schools were needed
to fulfill a distinctive Catholic vision of education the
bishops also clearly asserted the American identity of
the schools. In a break with the image of the Catholic
school system as a fortress defending ethnic and religious
enclaves from a dangerous and hostile environment, the
bishops stressed the public character and responsibilities
of Catholic schools.

> The school, therefore, whether private or
> public as regards maintenance and control,
> is an agency for social welfare, and as such
> it bears responsibility to the whole civic
> body.

They also challenged America's commitment to public schooling as the primary agency of civic formation, arguing that

---

[13](New York: Macmillan Co., 1921), pp. 37, 39.

"education that unites intellectual, moral and religious elements" offered "the best training for citizenship." The bishops concluded their pastoral letter with a declaration that became something of a battle cry in the defense of Catholic schools in the 1920's.

> Our Catholic schools are not established and maintained with any idea of holding our children apart from the general body and spirit of American citizenship. They are simply the concrete form in which we exercise our rights as free citizens, in conformity with the dictates of conscience. Their very existence is a great moral fact in American life. For while they aim, openly and avowedly, to preserve our Catholic faith, they offer to all our people an example of the use of freedom for the advancement of morality and religion.[14]

Underlying this understanding of the religious and social functions of the schools was an assumption of the basic compatibility, even the identity, of Catholic and American values and ideals. As one Catholic school apologist reasoned:

> No freedom is possible unless based on a moral, even a religious foundation . . . . The preservation of democracy is not only the task of education, but primarily of religious education . . . . Only a widespread acceptance of the doctrines, standards, and ideals of Christ can secure government of the people, by the people, and for the people. In other words, democratic living and Christian living are for practical purposes synonymous.[15]

Most Catholic educators saw little tension or conflict in their commitment to provide education that was both genuinely

---

[14]"Pastoral Letter," pp. 188, 190, 192.

[15]Ryan, "Religious Education and Democracy," p. 324.

Catholic and thoroughly American.   One CEA member proudly

testified.

> We are at once Catholic educators and American
> educators. As Catholic educators, we are re-
> sponsible to the Church for the safeguarding of
> our Catholic youth against the rampant irreli-
> gion and the corrupting immorality of the age
> . . . . On the other hand, we are American edu-
> cators, and as such, we are morally bound to
> render good service to our country. This we
> can do in a general way by cultivating a high
> feeling of patriotic pride and enthusiasm for
> whatever concerns the honor, the dignity, and
> the fair renown of our country among the nations.
> In particular, the moral obligation is upon all
> of us to inculcate in our pupils respect for
> and obedience to civil authority, ungrudging
> acceptance of the sanctions of civil law and
> the faithful discharge of the duties of the
> citizens.[16]

However, it was the "American" side of this equation

that critics most consistently questioned and Catholics

most vigorously defended.   Archbishop John Glennon of St. Louis

in 1919 claimed that the country's experience at war should

have put an end to criticism against "the religious sys-

tem of training."

> Our government . . . has long since passed
> away from the crude belief that a training
> in secular branches of education is all that
> an American citizen requires. It has found
> out through the war that secular training
> aided by military and scientific training
> may make an efficient, but not necessarily
> a willing, nor yet a reliable soldier--that
> he needs not alone hands trained to fight,
> but a heart for sacrifice, and a soul to
> throw into the defense of the cause he be-
> lieves to be just.

---

[16]Brother Bernardine, F.S.C., "Differentiation in
the Seventh and Eighth Grades: Viewpoint of Vocational
Preparation," CEA Bulletin 16 (November 1919):127.

To meet this deeper need, Glennon maintained the need
for a public "code of morals" requiring the "sanction of
religion" to insure "its acceptance and its faithful
performance." Thus he concluded:

> He is not a patriot who would declare that
> every school that teaches faith in Christ
> must be faithless to America; or that the one
> who denies the supremacy and completeness of
> purely secular training is an enemy of his
> country.[17]

Along similar lines, Henry Moeller insisted that the church
"has no apology to make for her labors in the field of
education" because "an education based upon and buttressed
by religion ensures the genuine happiness and the proper
prosperity of the State." Citizens would respect and obey
authority "when the strong conviction has taken root in
their souls that rulers and lawmakers are God's representatives" and "that disobedience incurs the displeasure of
their Heavenly Father."[18] Indeed, in Shahan's estimation,
democracy as a political system lacked

> in its uncertain relation to authority, the
> ready, willing obedience to self-imposed laws,
> and the support of social order and inequal-
> ities of various kinds that are or seem to
> be unavoidable, given human nature and its
> . . . history.

Catholicism could thus aid democracy because "more than
any other institution," it cultivated among men "the spirit

[17]"Opening Sermon," CEA Bulletin 16 (November 1919):45-46.

[18]"Sermon by Most Rev. Henry Moeller, D.D.," CEA
Bulletin 18 (November 1921):42-46.

and practice of self-sacrifice for the common good, without which no form of social order can long survive."[19]

The task of defending the "Americanism" of Catholic schools was the particular responsibility of the National Catholic Welfare Council's department of education and its executive secretary, James H. Ryan. One of the first tasks assigned to the department soon after its founding in 1920 was to prepare for the bishops a "Standard Apologetic for Catholic Educational Work" that would present the official "attitude, platform, and policy of the church on public, private, and parochial education"--stressing those things that would be "the best line of defense for Catholic schools in this country today."[20] As a result, Ryan in 1922 authored a pamphlet entitled The Catechism of Catholic Education that offered a comprehensive and systematic apologetic for Catholic schooling in the United States. Ryan reminded readers that "the first American schools were religious schools" while the tax supported public schools dated from the 1850's and had no claim "to being considered the only true American system of education." While identifying the "religious atmosphere" of the schools as their most prominent characteristic, Ryan maintained that "the curriculum . . . in the secular branches is practically the same as

[19]Thomas J. Shahan, "First General Session," CEA Bulletin 17 (November 1920):27.

[20]"Hierarchy Approves Work of Welfare Council," NCWC Bulletin 2 (October 1920):7.

that of the public school, including English as the basic
language of instruction.

> The Catholic schools in which the instruction
> is given wholly in a foreign language are very
> few and are becoming fewer every year. The
> policy of the Church . . . has not been to force
> the issue, but slowly to await the opportune
> time when each foreign group is prepared for
> the acceptance of the English language. In
> this way it has not offended the racial sensi-
> bilities of the immigrant and has succeeded
> in transforming the foreign language school
> . . . into a school where the English language
> is the sole medium of instruction.

In addition, Catholic schools prove their Americanism by

requiring all teachers to be American citizens and by teach-

ing "love and respect for America." He quoted approvingly

an editorial in the <u>Brooklyn Daily Eagle</u>.

> Long controversies have been waged in the past
> over church schools, but there is at least this
> to be said for them, that none of the young
> socialists and incipient revolutionists who are
> now seen as a danger received their training
> in such schools. The root of this revolutionary
> teaching is agnosticism or a thinly veiled
> atheism. Faith in God and reverence for God
> make for the respect and observance of moral and
> social law, and the need for religious training
> is seen clearly at a time when men and women
> go about seeking to overturn the foundation of
> the moral and social order.

While carefully denying that Catholics "opposed" public

schools, Ryan argued that neither Sunday nor vacation

schools, which most Catholics viewed as at best a "make-

shift" arrangement for religious education, nor public

schools, which could appeal only to "natural" motives in

promoting good citizenship could provide the kind of

education necessary to sustain the moral and civic foundations

of democracy. Only religious schools could "appeal to
the highest motives which are spiritual and religious" in
educating loyal and responsible citizens of the Republic.
Finally, Ryan pointed to the work of Catholic schools in
"Americanizing" the foreign-born as a major contribution
to the nation and proof that Catholic schools were deserv-
ing of public support.[21]

Catholic Schools and Americanization

The following description illustrates the double-edged
ideology supporting Catholic schools in the 1920's:

> Outside, the parish school is like any other
> schools; inside, there is a perfectly differ-
> ent atmosphere from the public school's, and
> yet there is no separation from the world
> . . . . No plan . . . meets more squarely the
> original and once unspoiled American idea of
> education as understood by the founders of the
> republic and still retained by plain, straight,
> old-fashioned Americans.[22]

While Catholic educators were confident of the religious
qualities of the schools, they were under severe pressure
to demonstrate that the schools were socially responsible.
As a result, school leaders gave a great deal of attention

---

[21]Excerpts from The Catechism of Catholic Education
were published serially in the NCWC Bulletin. "Reasons for
the Existence of the Catholic Schools," NCWC Bulletin 3
(September 1922):28-29; and "Americanism of the Catholic
School," NCWC Bulletin 3 (October 1922):32-34.

[22]Dunney, p. 26.

to the social and civic functions of Catholic schools
in the early 1920's.

In principle there was little disagreement among
national leaders that "Americanization" was a prominent
goal of Catholic schooling. The diocesan superintendent
of schools in Duluth, Minnesota in 1922 officially designated
parochial schools as "Public Catholic Schools" so that the
"American tone of Catholic education will be put more to
the fore."[23] The Pittsburgh superintendent in 1919 reported
that the church had a unique responsibility and opportunity
"to be a guiding force" in the Americanization movement.

> To strengthen our national life, to perpet-
> uate our liberties under the Constitution, to
> guard against insidious attacks upon republican
> institutions, we advocate a vigorous and holy
> spirit of Americanism in our schools, a deep and
> intelligent love of our institutions, reverence
> for our flag and respect for our laws. The
> lessons of patriotism based on religion should
> be made a part of our daily school life so that
> our educational system should maintain a strong
> national character and be a powerful aid to the
> true development of our national life and national
> ideals.[24]

Thomas Edward Shield, professor of education at Catholic
University, described Catholic education as the "basis of
true Americanization" because in addition to communicating
the basic skills and knowledge necessary for citizenship,
the schools cultivated the supernatural virtues that formed

---

[23]M'Clancy, "What the Superintendents are Doing," p. 593.

[24]"Pittsburgh School Report Emphasizes Civics and
Americanization," NCWC Bulletin 2 (December 1920):21.

a broad and deep foundation for loyal and active citizenship.[25]

John A. Lapp of the NCWC's Social Action department echoed

similar sentiments.

> The Catholic school, because of its emphasis upon
> religion as the animating motive of true citizen-
> ship, is one of the best agencies for training
> citizens. The Catholic school teaches justice,
> charity, fair play and obedience to proper author-
> ity. If these virtues are correlated with the
> civic life of the community, a powerful force
> for civic righteousness will be developed.[26]

Lapp, along with Charles A. McMahon, a layman with experience

in adult education, headed the Civic Education Bureau of

the Social Action Department which conducted a nationwide

civic education campaign aimed especially at the immigrant

in 1919. The Bureau promoted "free public entertainments"

and "community houses" offering movies, talks on the duties

of citizenship and the naturalization process, counseling

on vocational opportunities, advice on health, sanitation

and safety measures, and instruction in the English language.[27]

The NCWC also began to encourage Catholic participation

in Boy Scouts, long considered a "Protestant" organization,

because it developed citizens "who know one ism, who love

---

[25]"Catholic Education: The Basis of True Americanization," CER 19 (January 1921):3-19.

[26]"Unite Courses in Civic and Social Problems,"
NCWC Bulletin 5 (September 1923):7.

[27]See Charles A. McMahon, "The NCWC Program for
Better Citizenship," NCWC Bulletin 3 (September 1921):6;
John A. Lapp, "The Campaign for Civic Instruction," NCWC
Bulletin 1 (July 1919):11-12; "Citizenship Taught Through
Motion Pictures," NCWC Bulletin 1 (August 1919):9-13; and
"A Model Citizenship Program," NCWC Bulletin 1 (February
1920):11-12.

one ism, and who profess one ism--100% AMERICANISM."[28]
Their most far-reaching effort, however was the publication
and distribution of over one million copies of The
Fundamentals of Citizenship, a pamphlet explaining the work-
ings of democracy. The text was also issued in question
and answer form as the Civics Catechism on the Rights and
Duties of American Citizens, which was subsequently trans-
lated into fourteen foreign languages, introduced into
Catholic schools throughout the country, published serially
in the Catholic and foreign language press, and used as
a text in adult Americanization programs.[29]

The task of "Americanization" also became a major
focus of discussion and reflection at annual CEA meetings
in the twenties as numerous speakers offered proposals
for courses, programs and approaches to promote patriotism
and citizenship education in parochial schools.[30] In 1920
the parish school department passed a resolution to include
courses in American patriotism along lines suggested by

[28]Francis A. Kelley, "Defenders of Our Democracy,"
NCWC Bulletin 1 (June-July 1920):6.

[29]See Charles A. McMahon, "Education and Good
Citizenship," NCWC Bulletin (March-April 1920):14-17; and Lapp,
"Unite Courses," pp. 79.

[30]For example, see Mary Adelaide, "Practical Civic
Training, General and Local," CEA Bulletin 18 (November 1921):
323-42: John B. Peterson, "Education for Citizenship in Christ's
Kingdom," CEA Bulletin 23 (November 1926):42-51; and Daniel
J. Feeney, "Preparing Pupils for Conservative Leadership in
Civic Affairs," CEA Bulletin 25 (November 1928):352-62.

the NCWC in all parochial schools.[31] While many schools
continued to function as national or ethnic schools well
beyond the 1920's, the policy of the CEA was clearly to
promote the image of "American Catholic" schools. The
general body of the CEA in 1919 passed a resolution calling
for the teaching of English in all Catholic schools in
the country[32] and the issue of "ethnicity" was not even
mentioned at any national meeting during the 1920's or 30's.

Although committed in theory to "Americanization"
as a goal of Catholic schooling, Catholic educators held a
fairly wide range of views on the nature, purpose and means
of achieving this goal. The predominant view seemed to
be a moderate position advocating a "melting pot" theory of
gradual, but deliberate assimilation. These educators, while
urging the church to become more active in encouraging ethnic
assimilation, were also critical of the extremism of the
Americanization movement, especially the use of coercive
methods, denigration of the immigrant's foreign background,
and demands for the immediate abandonment of all old world
ties, including the exclusive use of the English language.
Representing this view, Bishop Turner of Buffalo in 1923
told a Knights of Columbus audience that the church

> does not believe in insulting the immigrants
> racial pride in order to make them Americans

---

[31]"Parish School Department," CEA Bulletin 17 (November
1920):178.

[32]"Parish School Department," CEA Bulletin 16 (November
1919):250.

and deplores the devices of others, devices
conceived in hysteria and applied in petulancy
and passion, that would force on our immigrant
population the superficial traits of citizenship,
neglecting the essentials.[33]

The official attitude of the NCWC in general also followed
this moderate position. John Lapp, in a study of the
Pittsburgh diocese schools, recommended to the school superintendent that Catholic schools

should insist upon the teaching of the English
language and American civic ideals to all children,
but without preventing instruction in the language
of the old home-land and instruction in the patriotic
and civic ideals of their old home-country . . . .
All that helps to strengthen American Democracy
out of the aspirations of the democracies of Poland,
Bohemia, Hungary, Italy and other countries should
be utilized.[34]

Lapp, like his colleague John Ryan at the NCWC Social
Action department, was one of a small number of Catholic
social reconstructionists who offered a more radical critique
against the class and cultural imposition of Americanization
efforts and proposed different goals for similar Catholic
programs. Lapp charged that though ostensibly committed
to promoting patriotism, "Americanization" was used as a
"rampart for reactionary wealth and privileges" and was
often "directed toward the discrediting of progressive
measures for social justice, and particularly the destruction of the organization of labor." He argued that

no plan short of complete social justice should
be held as a goal for good citizenship or

[33]"Education of Catholic Children," NCWC Bulletin 6
(September 1924):3.

[34]"Pittsburg School Report," p. 7.

> Americanization . . . . loyalty and devotion
> to American institutions can be promoted best
> by the prevention of exploitation of the weak
> by the strong or crafty; by the promotion of
> justice in the distribution of the world's income;
> by the development of moral purpose; and by
> the molding of our institutions to promote these
> ends.[35]

William J. McAuliffe of Cathedral College in New York City likewise insisted that "any problem of Americanization that is worth anything must be satisfactory to the worker."[36]

Another group of Catholic educators who were unabashedly assimilationist had few reservations about full and speedy "Americanization" and recommended that Catholic schools be organized and operated to accomplish this end. Brooklyn school superintendent Joseph V. S. M'Clancy urged Catholic schools to join in

> the endeavor to make América a united people,
> to eliminate alienism and radicalism, to turn
> out of our lower schools boys and girls, the
> men and women of tomorrow, who will shed all
> foreign tastes and allegiance and come into
> the unity of a nation, one in language, admir-
> ation and action.

To accomplish this "noble project," M'Clancy recommended that all Catholic teachers have full citizenship; that the atmosphere of Catholic schools be made "intensely American" through classroom decorations and daily displays of the American flag; that English be the sole language of instruction; that history and civics be taught so as to develop "a

---

[35]"Bogus Propaganda: Dollar Mark Shows in Attempts to Control Americanization Program," NCWC Bulletin 1 (June–July 1920):9.

[36]"The Problem of Americanization," CEA Bulletin 16 (November 1919):186.

burning love and admiration for America"; and that schools
schedule daily patriotic exercises and national as well
as religious holidays. He also encouraged Catholic schools
to adopt courses of study parallel to those of the public
schools and urged more cordial relations between the two
systems.

> While we are committed to religious education
> it is well to remember that others are content
> with a secular education, reinforced by Sunday
> school and home teaching of religion. We are
> doing much harm to Catholic education when we
> pursue a policy of unwarranted criticism of any
> system of education other than our own.[37]

Finally conservative educators committed to Catholicism
as a total cultural reality felt that the social and "this
worldly" focus of Americanization efforts were counter to
Catholic educational principles. Charles A. Baschab, a
professor at Dominican College in California, in 1927 warned
CEA members that Catholic schools in the U.S. were "in
imminent danger of intellectual perversion" from socialistic
and nationalistic tendencies. According to Catholic principles,
argued Baschab, educational goals should be determined first
by the needs of the individual, then the family, and only
then by the interests of the state and nation. An over-
emphasis on Americanization he warned had caused Catholic
schools to reverse these priorities.[38] John B. Peterson,

---

[37]"Americanization and Catholic Elementary Schools,"
CEA Bulletin 16 (November 1919):252-60.

[38]"The State and Education," CEA Bulletin 24 (November
1927):40-48.

president of St. John's Seminary in Brighton, Massachusetts, flatly denied that "a working theory of government by social contract" was at all tenable and insisted Catholic educators should concentrate instead on training citizens for Christ's kingdom.[39]

Critics of Americanization as a goal of Catholic schools were in the minority in national policy discussions in the 1920's. However, they were perhaps most representative of the views of newly arrived immigrants committed to a position of cultural pluralism. According to historian Mark Linkh, these immigrants continued to use national parishes and foreign language parochial schools to retain cultural ties with their former homeland. When these were unavailable, the foreign-born often chose to attend public schools with multi-ethnic constituencies rather than English-language parochial schools that seemed more aggressively "American" than Catholic.[40]

In summary, the following themes dominated the ideology of Catholic schooling in the 1920's:

1. Catholic schools as a leaven for the transformation of American culture.
2. Catholic schools as the most authentic expression of the American educational ideal.

---

[39]Peterson, p. 49.

[40]"Catholicism and the European Immigrant, 1900-1924: A Chapter in American Catholic Social Thought," (Ed.D. dissertation, Teachers College, Columbia University, 1973) pp. 299-306.

3. The uniqueness of Catholic schools based upon a "permeation theory" of the relation between religion and education.

4. The compatibility of "Americanism" and "Catholicism."

5. Religious education as a foundation for democratic
   living.

6. The equivalence of Catholic schools and public schools
   in secular subjects.

7. Catholic schools as agencies of Americanization.

This understanding of the role and purposes of Catholic
schooling represents a significant shift of emphasis from
the defensive, isolationist mentality supporting the founding of Catholic schools in the United States. As Robert
O'Gorman has observed, though the structure of isolation
(the rival school system) and the church's intention to
control Catholics' relation to culture was maintained into
the twentieth century, "Americanization" (the ideal of making
Catholic schools equally effective producers of Americans
as the public schools) replaced the nineteenth century goals
of creating a pure Catholic culture or of aligning Catholicism with its various ethnic expressions.[41] However, the
attempt to create an educational synthesis of "American"
and "Catholic" traditions did not completely resolve differences over the proper relationship of Catholic faith to
American culture as school leaders continued to maintain
divergent social views, each claiming to represent the
authentic American Catholic position.

---

[41]O'Gorman, pp. 137-38.

Chapter IV

DEFENDING THE SCHOOLS

The early 1920's marked a watershed in the development
of Catholic schooling in the United States. Having become
fully committed to the ideal of "every Catholic child in
a Catholic school" as a matter of religious principle, U.S.
Catholics faced the possibility that public pressure and
hostile legislation could inflict serious damage or even
bring about the destruction of the Catholic school system.
Defense of the schools became an overriding national
priority as church leaders mounted a massive campaign to
protect the integrity and independence of Catholic schools
in American society.

Catholic Schools and the State

Because of church-state hostilities in Europe, conservative Roman Catholic leaders in the nineteenth century
had come to view the state as an opponent rather than an
ally of the church. In the United States with its strong
tradition of anti-Catholicism, church leaders had embraced
the doctrine of separation of church and state as affording
Catholics protection against undue government interference
in religious affairs. Thus it was not surprising that
Catholic church leaders had grave misgivings about the expansion of the role and function of government in the U.S.

after World War I. In 1919 the conservative archbishop of
Boston, William O'Connell, called for "reasonable limits"
to state authority. Opposing the "desire for centralizing
control," O'Connell warned the Catholic Educational Association that the United States was "drifting away from democratic government and trespassing upon the rights and liberties of the citizens" especially in the area of education
and was "assuming functions never anticipated and never in-
tended when the Constitution was written." Reiterating
traditional Catholic teaching, O'Connell insisted that in
matters pertaining to religion or morals, the church has
supreme authority, while the state's role is but to "encourage and protect" and "to act only when such action is demanded by the good of the community and only after private
initiative has proved inadequate to cope with the situation."
The protection of the rights of individuals, families and
the church "makes imperative in the State a tendency towards
decentralization rather than toward centralization of power."[1]
An editorial in the Catholic Education Review the following
year protested that however justified during "the stress
and strain of war, . . . the centralization of control in
the National Government . . . is nothing less than unmitigated
calamity in times of peace," particularly when "it reaches
its evil hand and touches the education of our children."[2]

---

[1]"The Reasonable Limits of State Activity," CEA
Bulletin 16 (November 1919):63-72.

[2]Thomas Edward Shields, CER 18 (April 1920):214.

94

Even more strongly worded apprehensions were echoed by
the NCWC administrative board in an official release prepared by general secretary John Burke in 1922:

> The growth of bureaucracy in the United States
> is one of the most significant after-effects
> of the war. This growth must be resolutely
> checked. Federal assistance and federal direc-
> tion are in some cases beneficial and even
> necessary but extreme bureaucracy is foreign
> to everything American. It is unconstitutional
> and undemocratic. It means officialism, red
> tape and prodigal waste of public money. It
> spells hordes of so-called experts and self-
> perpetuating cliques of politicians to regulate
> every detail of life. It would eventually
> sovietize our form of government.[3]

However, at a time when such views were often regarded
as _prima facie_ evidence of the incompatibility of "Romanism"
and true "Americanism," there was another more conciliatory
Catholic attitude toward the state that was also to significantly influence Catholic school policies and practices.
In the late nineteenth century, church leaders such as
Bishop John Ireland and theologian Thomas Bouquillon pro-
voked intense controversy with the suggestion that the
state had rights independent of the church in education
and that public schools that separate the teaching of
religion from education were tolerable under certain circumstances. Despite the implied rejection of such views by
Pope Leo XIII's condemnation of "Americanism," the U.S.
bishops in 1919 adopted essentially the same position
in their pastoral letter to the U.S. church. The bishops
acknowledged the state's right to conduct schools and to

[3]Cited by Hennesey, _American Catholics_, p. 248.

set minimum educational standards "to safeguard its vital
interests against the dangers that result from ignorance,"
as well as "the duty to exclude the teaching of doctrines
which aim at the subversion of law and order and therefore
at the destruction of the State itself." Whether publicly
or privately controlled, all schools, insisted the bishops,
have the duty to adhere to these standards to fulfill their
social and civic responsibilities. However, they also maintained that the state did not have the right to usurp the
prior rights of the parents to choose religious schooling
for their children, "so long as these rights are properly
exercised" and could not compel attendance at state-run
schools.[4]

In seeking theological support for this position
Catholic apologists referred to the "two kingdoms" analysis
of church-state relations developed by Leo XIII in his
encyclical "On the Christian Constitution of States."

> The almighty has appointed the charge of the
> human race between two powers, the ecclesiasti-
> cal and the civil, the one being set over
> divine, the other over human things. Each in
> its kind is supreme, each has fixed limits
> within which it is contained, limits which
> are defined by the nature and special object
> of the province of each, so that there is,
> we may say, an orbit traced out within which
> the action of each is brought into play by its
> own native right.[5]

---

[4]"Pastoral Letter," pp. 189-92.

[5]Quoted in John A. Ryan, The Catholic Church and
the Citizen (New York: Macmillan, 1928), p. 24.

John A. Ryan, the outstanding Catholic social theorist of
the period, in particular, sought to reinterpret some of
the more illiberal and ultramontanist assertions of the
encyclical to show how

> there can be no genuine conflict between
> proper loyalty to the state and proper
> loyalty to any other society whether it be
> the Church, the family or some private
> association.[6]

By carefully delineating the respective rights and responsibilities of church and state in education and then virtually
denying the possibility of any real conflict, Catholic
theology prepared the ground for the church's gradual
acceptance of an expanded, though still limited governmental
role in education.

The NCWC: Organizing a Defense

The spectre of government intervention in education
at the end of World War I impressed Catholic leaders with
the importance of being able to mount an effective, organized response to any external threat to Catholic schools.
It was with this end in view that the American bishops in
September 1920 approved plans for a department of education in the newly formed National Catholic Welfare Council.
Under the episcopal leadership of Archbishop Austin Dowling
of St. Paul, chairman; the Rev. James H. Ryan, executive
secretary; and an executive committee composed of sixteen

---

[6]Ibid. See chapter 3, "Conflicting Loyalties--
Church and State," pp. 23-46.

prominent Catholic educators, the department was to serve
as a "clearing house of information concerning Catholic
education," "an advisory agency" to assist the development
of the Catholic school system, "a connecting agency" between Catholic schools and government agencies affecting
education, and "an active organization" committed to safe-
guarding Catholic school interests.[7]

The National Catholic Welfare Council represented
a significant departure from the traditional pattern of
leadership in the American Catholic community. Throughout
the nineteenth century, mutual distrust and suspicion among
members of the hierarchy based on ethnic differences and
disagreements over how the church should relate to American
society prevented any successful attempts at organizing
Catholic activities on a national level. World War I,
however, brought about a remarkable consensus among the
U.S. bishops, conservatives and liberals,

---

[7]"Opening of NCWC Bureau of Education," NCWC Bulletin
2 (February 1921):9-10. The original members of the execu-
tive committee, in addition to Dowling and Ryan, were
Thomas J. Shahan, D.D., Rector, Catholic University of America;
James A. Burns, C.S.C., President, University of Notre Dame;
John P. Chidwick, D.D., President, St. Joseph's Seminary in
New York; John A. Dillon, Diocesan Superintendent of Newark,
New Jersey parochial schools; John F. Fenlon, D.D., President,
Divinity College, Catholic University; Albert C. Fox, S.J.,
President, Campion College; Francis W. Howard, LLD, Secretary,
Catholic Education Association; Francis T. Moran, pastor, St.
Patrick's Church; Edward A. Pace, Ph.D., General Secretary,
Catholic University; John B. Peterson, D.D., Rector, St. John's
Seminary, Boston; Brother G. Philip, President, St. Thomas College;
Joseph Smith, New York Diocesan Superintendent of Schools; R. H.
Tierney, S.J., editor, America; John A. Waldron, S.M.; Francis
Walsh, Vice-Rector, Mt. St. Mary's Seminary of the West; and
John J. Wynne, S.J., Encyclopedia Press. "The NCWC Explained,"
NCWC Bulletin 3 (January 1922):19.

on the justice of the American cause, the
need to actively embrace the principal virtues of Catholicism in order to win American
goals, and the practical identification of
Americanism and Christianity.[8]

This unified national outlook provided a basis for the

organization of the National Catholic War Council in 1917

in response to government requests for church assistance

in the war. The NCWC's success at organizing Catholic

support for the war won national prominence for the church

and persuaded many U.S. bishops of the value of a strong

organizational base for the church's activities as well

as inspiring among them a new measure of confidence in

the ability and even obligation of the church to exert

influence in public affairs.[9] Despite considerable resis-

tance to this centralization after the war, most of the

hierarchy approved the forming of the National Catholic

Welfare Council in 1919 to continue coordinating Catholic

activities on a national basis in peace time and to provide

"united, coordinated and militant action" for the "protection

and defense of the Church in America, its institutions, its

teachings and its lawful rights."[10]

---

[8]McKeown, p. 80.

[9]Ibid., *passim*; and Hennesey, *American Catholics*, pp. 226-
228, 243-46.

[10]"Around the Council Table," *NCWC Bulletin* 5 (July 1923):
14. A few conservative churchmen led by Philadelphia Cardinal
Doughtery and Boston Cardinal O'Connell in 1922 convinced Roman
authorities that the NCWC represented a potential threat to
papal authority and was a source of division in the U.S. church
and thus secured a papal decree suppressing the NCWC and banning
annual meetings of the U.S. bishops. An appeal by the NCWC administrative committee and protestations of support by the bishops

To those Catholics fearful that a national organization would interfere with local autonomy or supercede the jurisdiction of individual bishops, the NCWC was careful to clarify its specific and limited role.

> It is not, as some of the Catholic journals
> of the country reported, a centralization of
> authority. It is the unification of Catholic
> effort. It is the ability to bring the immense
> Catholic resources into common activity when
> needed. It is a bureau that will be not the
> master, but the servant of the Catholic activi-
> ties and organizations of the country . . . .
> We are wasting our efforts and our opportuni-
> ties if, through lack of unity and conference,
> our voice in matters of public concern expresses
> one opinion in one place and another in another
> place.[11]

Many Catholics harbored similar suspicions in regard to the work of the department of education. James H. Ryan, disclaimed any intentions on the part of the bishops to create "a sort of national educational super government." He insisted that the department's functions were "purely advisory and directive" and that "no effort will be made to control the Catholic schools of the United States."[12] On the other hand, he stressed the department's importance in molding a unified Catholic educational point of view.

----

led Rome to rescind its decree. The NCWC was rein-
stated as the National Catholic Welfare Conference to indicate the organization's lack of canonical authority over
individual bishops.

[11]"The National Catholic Welfare Council," NCWC
Bulletin 1 (January 1920):7-8.

[12]"Policy of NCWC Educational Department Stated,"
NCWC Bulletin 3 (September 1921):26.

> If our Catholic school system is eventually
> to reach its natural development and to exert
> on American public life the influence it
> should, it will only be when every Catholic
> teacher, from New York to San Francisco learns
> to think, to speak, and to act as a great national
> Catholic unity.[13]

Concerning its relation to the Catholic Educational Association, Thomas J. Shahan, president general of the CEA, announced that the establishment of the NCWC department of education brought the CEA "into closer association with the Catholic hierarchy," the effect of which would be to help define "more clearly our educational policy," "secure greater unity and consistency in our endeavors," and "give the sanction of authority to all proposals and resolutions approved by the Department."[14]

When plans for the work of the education department were formally approved, the threat of hostile legislation was clearly a main concern. The U.S. bishops assigned the department the task of outlining

> a policy on the position of the Church in
> educational matters with a view to meeting
> situations like those which have arisen in
> Michigan and Nebraska and in the Smith-
> Towner Bill, as well as in other forms of
> opposition to Catholic educational interests,
> and to carry on a propaganda by means of
> pamphlets and lectures to further these same
> ends.

Committed to defending Catholic education, but fearful that aggressive political action would unduly antagonize the

---

[13]"4000 Catholic Teachers Learn of NCWC Educational Department," NCWC Bulletin 3 (September 1921):27.

[14]"Address of Rt. Rev. Thomas J. Shahan, D.D.," CEA Bulletin 17 (November 1920):28. The CEA however, "maintained independence and continued free to speak without

public, the bishops accepted the NCWC executive committee's recommendation that

> in defining the Catholic attitude towards
> measures for State and Federal control,
> Catholics should give the minimum of com-
> plaint and of opposition to such movements.
> They should discriminate between the things
> they can accept and those which they cannot
> accept--and then confine their opposition
> to the latter.[15]

This policy established the foundation of a new relation between Catholic schools and the state in the 1920's. Catholics would in no way compromise on any issue threatening the existence of Catholic schools. Thus the church stood unanimously and officially opposed to two major issues--the creation of a federal department of education and compulsory public school attendance laws. However, to further insure the continued rights of Catholic schools to exist, Catholic educational leaders were willing to accept a larger role for the state in setting educational standards in the conduct of Catholic schools.

authority and consequently without commitment of the Hierarchy" according to Anne B. Whitmer and F. G. Hochwalt, former secretary general of the NCEA in "The National Catholic Educational Association: 1903-1951," Catholic School Journal 51 (April 1951):127.

[15]"Hierarchy Approves Work of Welfare Council," p. 7.

Opposing Federalization

The U.S. bishops in their 1919 pastoral letter had
laid the foundation for Catholic opposition to the efforts
to establish a federal department of education in the 1920's.
Referring to the growing clamor for social reform through
legislative means, the bishops cautioned against multiplying
"laws and restrictions." The ideal of democracy, they insisted,was for all citizens "to live in harmony under the
simplest possible form, and only the necessary amount of
external regulation." The common good could only be achieved
on "a sure foundation in the individual mind and conscience."
Rather than through social legislation, the hierarchy concluded that "it is mainly through education that our country
will accomplish its task and perpetuate its free institutions."[16]
Voluntarism, local control of decision-making, the improvement of society through virtuous individuals and the
ameliorative effects of education were the hallmarks of
this Catholic social vision.

Nevertheless, initial Catholic reactions to proposed
Congressional legislation to create a cabinet-level depart-
ment providing federal aid to public schools were mixed.
In response to an inquiry by Cardinal Gibbons of Baltimore,
Monsignor Edward A. Pace, vice-rector of the Catholic
University, stated that the provision of proposed legislation

---

[16]"Pastoral Letter," pp. 184-85.

denying federal monies to private and parochial schools would give public schools significant advantages over Catholic schools. The measure, he added, might lend support to efforts to compel children to attend public schools. On the positive side, Pace anticipated that centralized educational authority might help to eliminate discrimination by establishing standards by which Catholic schools might qualify for federal assistance. Gibbons himself was undecided in the matter. Though fearing that the measure would "put an entering wedge involving the rights of Catholics in the matter of education," he ceded that in the interest of protecting Catholic schools

> it would be more satisfactory to deal with a few intelligent men in Washington than is the case now where we have to deal with so many petty, narrow officials of each state.[17]

At Pace's urging, Gibbons appointed a committee to evaluate the matter and make their recommendations available to the bishops for official consideration at their annual meeting in September 1919. After consultation on the matter, the bishops concluded that the dangers from "federalization" to Catholic schools far outweighed any possible benefits and in 1920 the National Catholic Welfare Council went on record opposing the proposal before Congress, the Smith-Towner Bill. While expressing

---

[17] John Tracy Ellis, The Life of James Cardinal Gibbons, Archbishop of Baltimore 1834-1921, 2 vols. (Milwaukee: Bruce Publishing Co., 1952), 2:543-45.

approval of the educational purposes the bill was designed
to aid--the elimination of illiteracy, Americanization of
immigrants, improved health and safety standards, and teacher
preparation--the NCWC offered six basic objects to the proposed method of extending federal aid to the states. First,
the bill represented "another step towards centralization"
by placing states in the financial debt of the federal
government. Second, by creating dependency on the federal
government, the bill would destroy the states' autonomy in
educational matters. Third, it would constitute an unfair
use of appropriations from more prosperous states to aid
education in less prosperous states. Fourth, by shifting
educational responsibilities to the federal government,
states would lose interest in supporting public education.
Fifth, by creating the position of Secretary of Education
to be filled by political appointment, the measure would
politicize education as succeeding administrations used
the educational system to further their own partisan interests. Finally, the bishops concluded that

> with the present national debt, enormous
> taxes and the cost of all commodities, it
> would certainly be unwise for Congress to
> lay an extra burden of one hundred million
> dollars annually on the people at large.[18]

James Ryan in the department of education criticized
the measure as an attempt to create a national system of
schools.

---

[18]"Welfare Council Issues Statement on the Smith-Towner
Bill," p. 24.

To nationalize education is to centralize it,
and to that extent, undemocratize it. What
education needs to-day is not more, but less,
centralization. Educational salvation is not
to be found in the office of a secretary in
the President's Cabinet, nor will it ever be
purchased by subsidies granted from Washington.
Democratic education, both in its administration
and in its aims, is a local matter. If it is
ever to accomplish the obligations of a democratic citizenship, the local character of the
school must never be relinquished. Each community
must see its duty and must be willing to embrace
the obligations consequent thereon, must jealously
guard its right to train its own children according to standards which it can understand and accept,
and not according to standards imposed by a benevo-
lent bureaucracy situated a thousand miles away.[19]

Following the NCWC's lead, the Catholic Educational

Association passed a resolution opposing Smith-Towner "or

any measure which tends to centralize at Washington powers

reserved under the Constitution to the respective States or

to the people."[20] William D. Guthrie, professor of Consti-

tutional Law at Columbia University, argued before the CEA

that Congress did not have the constitutional power to

regulate or control education in the manner proposed by

Smith-Towner.[21] The Central Bureau of the Central Society

of St. Louis printed and distributed free leaflets detail-

ing Catholic objections to Smith-Towner. Labeling the

proposal "an experiment in state socialism," the pamphlet

---

[19]"The Proposed Monopoly in Education," Atlantic Monthly
(February 1924), p. 178.

[20]CEA Bulletin 17 (November 1920):33.

[21]"The Federal Government and Education," CEA Bulletin 17
(November 1920):36.

objected to the bill's

> false assumption that none but the public
> schools have a right to exist and to oper-
> ate . . . the term public education must be
> applied to all education carried on in a
> free republic for the benefit of the people.

The pamphlet also pointed to the "grave danger that positive Christianity will not only be ignored but indirectly
combatted in the schools" with control of education in the
hands of federal bureaucrats.[22]

While united in their opposition to federalization,
Catholic leaders were divided on how aggressively to pursue
their protest against proposed Congressional legislation.
Having issued a public statement against Smith-Towner in
1920, the NCWC department of education issued a circular
letter suggesting that "protest be discontinued and opportunity given to study the situation developing under the
new Congress."[23]

After the defeat of Smith-Towner in 1920, similar
measures were introduced in succeeding Congressional sessions
in the 1920's.[24] As it became clear that support for the

[22]"For the Freedom of Education," reprinted in CER 18
(June 1920):332-53.

[23]"The National Catholic Welfare Conference Explained,"
NCWC Bulletin 3 (January 1922):20.

[24]See "Federal Subsidy of Education," NCWC Bulletin
5 (December 1920):14; James H. Ryan, "The Dallinger Education
Bill," NCWC Bulletin 5 (March 1924):9-10; and Idem, "Menace
of the Curtis-Reed 'Education Bill,'" NCWC Bulletin 7 (March
1926):7.

creation of a federal department of education was steadily
losing ground, most Catholic leaders saw little wisdom in
continuing vigorous public protest. The·U.S. bishops at
their annual meeting in 1925 decided "to make no propaganda"
against new education bills unless serious developments
made stronger action necessary.[25]

Not all Catholic leaders approved of this retreat.
An editorial in America, the Jesuit weekly, in 1926 warned
against "guardians of our Catholic interests" who would
betray the Church by easing its defenses. Archbishop Curley
of Baltimore wanted a more vigorous counterattack. Cardinal
O'Connell of Boston opposed Dowling's handling of educational
legislation for the NCWC, complaining that his lack of
Roman education "led him and men like him to surrender un-
knowingly on matters of principle."[26]

Despite the bishops earlier decision, the NCWC administrative committee decided to actively oppose the Curtis-
Reed Bill to institute federal supervision and aid to education in 1926. Their success in helping to defeat the
measure, according to John Burke, "set back federal education for years to come."[27]

------

[25]John B. Sheerin, Never Look Back: The Career and
Concerns of John J. Burke (New York: Paulist Press, 1975),
p. 99.

[26]Hennesey, American Catholics, p. 249; and Sheerin,
p. 100.

[27]Sheerin, p. 100.

Though the church's position opposing the "federalization" of education was consistent with its commitment to
voluntarism and local initiative expressed in the bishops'
1919 pastoral letter, it was clearly not in line with the
direction of the U.S. church's own internal organizational
revolution well underway by 1920. While arguing in principle
against centralization and bureaucracy in American social
life, Catholic leaders were at the same time forced to defend
against similar criticisms of the NCWC, an organization some
Catholics viewed as a "reflection of this burgeoning federal
regulation," "a bureaucratic colossus grasping for a
monopoly of ecclesiastical power."[28] While denying that
the NCWC represented any "centralization of authority,"
defenders of the organization argued that the church's
interests would best be served by the ability to match in
kind the expanded political influence and organization of
its opponents.[29] The Catholic Educational Association and
the National Conference of Catholic Charities were only
the first of a variety of organizations formed in the first
quarter of the twentieth century to encourage coordination
and more efficient organization of Catholic efforts and
resources on a national basis. The 1918 Code of Canon
Law legislated more uniform procedures in the conduct of

---

[28]These criticisms were noted by Michael Williams, founder
of the lay Catholic journal, Commonweal, in a letter to John
Burke in 1922. See Sheerin, pp. 85-86.

[29]For example, Archbishop Austin Dowling urged the U.S.
hierarchy to strengthen the role of the NCWC department of education to deal more effectively with threats to Catholic schools
from the Smith-Towner bill. See Ellis, The Life of Gibbons, 2:545

U.S. church life and stimulated the growth of centralized
administration within a more highly organized diocesan
church structure.[30] The development of the office of superintendent of education in dioceses across the country by 1920
was shifting educational responsibilities away from pastors
and principals as schools came under tighter diocesan
scrutiny and supervision. These developments were evidence
of a gradual recognition, however reluctant, by the U.S.
hierarchy of the inadequacies of local control and decentralization in developing a sense of internal cohesiveness in
the American Catholic community, gaining a position of influence in the larger society, and defending against attacks
from powerful and organized opponents. While basing their
arguments against federal control of education in the 1920's
in part on a principled opposition to bureaucracy and centralized decision-making in the organization of social life,
Catholic leaders in their choice of organizational strategy
embraced the very social forces they so vigorously sought
to restrain in the larger society. Power rather than
principle was the real issue as Catholic leaders, more pragmatic than ideological, sought to preserve and protect the
interests of Catholic schools.

---

[30]O'Brien, "Some Reflections on the Catholic Experience,"
pp. 13-16.

Opposing State Monopoly of Education

One reason for Catholics' vigorous opposition to a greater federal role in education was the incipient threat that expanded governmental authority would be used against Catholic schools, leading eventually to a state monopoly of education in the United States. Such fears were not totally unfounded in view of legislation inimical to Catholic schools under consideration in several states in the early 1920's including Washington, Ohio, Michigan and Nebraska. However, Oregon was the first state to be successful in outlawing Catholic elementary schools with the passage of a compulsory public school attendance law in November, 1922. The measure required parents, under pain of fine, imprisonment, or both, to send their children between the ages of eight and sixteen to public schools until they graduated from eighth grade unless they were physically unable, lived at too great a distance, or received a county superintendent's permission for private tutoring.[31]

Oregon's initiative became a focus for nationwide fears and concerns in the 1920's over "the perils of pluralism" in a democratic society and the limits and purposes of public schooling in maintaining social unity. At issue was the legitimacy of what one critic called "the dissociated schools" at a time when public schools were being held

---

[31]Tyack, "The Perils of Pluralism," p. 76.

responsible for eradicating "ideological and ethnic pluralism" in the interests of Americanism, sustaining traditional religious beliefs from evolutionary and historical modes of thought, and preserving reverential loyalty toward the nation from muckraking critics.[32] Supporters of the school law, including the Scottish Rite Masons and the Ku Klux Klan, appealed to the ideology of common schools, fear of immigrants, and anti-Catholicism in their successful campaign to insure that all children would be educated in public schools "along standardized lines" to "enable them to acquire a uniform outlook on all national and patriotic questions."[33] In maintaining their own private schools, Catholics were accused of plotting to "destroy all our public schools." One advertisement in a local Oregon newspaper warned that with "no defense against any private ideas antagonistic to our free institutions," children in Catholic schools were "being fitted to promote un-American ideals," many of whom would

> become subjects of a foreign prince, consciously or unconsciously, as his American agents--spies and traitors to the best interests of the United States.[34]

This direct attack on the existence of Catholic schooling in Oregon was universally condemned by Catholic leaders.

---

[32] Ibid., p. 75.

[33] Ibid., p. 77. The quote is from the Scottish Rite Masons' journal, New Age.

[34] Ibid., p. 85.

Archbishop Austin Dowling, episcopal chairman of the NCWC
education department, compared the law to the "Soviet claim
to invade the home and substitute communal for parental
care." Archbishop Michael J. Curley claimed that the "whole
trend of such legislation is state socialism setting up an
omnipotent state . . . on the principles of Karl Marx."[35]
A general resolution by the Catholic Educational Association
claimed that parish school education was not a "privilege"
but a "fundamental right"; and to suppress such schools
would be "a denial . . . of the principle of personal freedom itself."[36]

While the main issue for supporters of compulsory
public schooling was the maintenance of social cohesion,
Catholic opponents defined the issue as a referendum on
the rights of individual conscience and freedom of religious
expression. These two differing ideological positions
were well stated in an exchange of views in the Atlantic
Monthly between Cornelia James Cannon and James H. Ryan
on the nature and purposes of schooling in the education
of citizens for life in a democratic society. Cannon's
essay, "The Dissociated School," identified educational
separatism as a significant political and social problem
in the United States.

---

[35]Quoted in Jorgenson, pp. 458-59.

[36]"General Resolutions," CEA Bulletin 22 (November
1925):40.

> Is America, which has held the public or demo-
> cratic school equal in importance to liberty and
> justice for all, as prerequisite to her very exis-
> tence, ready to betray the one God, and erect many
> brazen idols in his place?
> The spread of private and sectarian schools
> in this country . . . has gone along with a very
> great increase in the proportion of citizens
> of alien traditions and customs in our midst.
> The withdrawal from the public schools of more
> and more of the children of those already Ameri-
> canized greatly enhances the difficulty of making
> a unit of this inchoate mass of human beings that
> we call America. What does such a shift of large
> numbers of children signify? One can think of
> it only as the recrudescence in this country of the
> aristocratic, sectarian, exclusive traditions
> of the older European civilizations--attitudes
> incompatible with belief in democracy, with group-
> ings determined by individual ability and capacity
> independent of inherited class or religious asso-
> ciations.
> Are not these groups of children set apart for
> reasons antagonistic to the purposes, and inimical
> to the upbuilding, of a democracy?

Cannon claimed that at the base of this "apostasy" were "three

types of human exclusiveness" historically used to justify

non-public forms of schooling. Parochial schools based on

"religious exclusiveness," according to Cannon,

> cannot fail to be narrowing. However noble the
> religious ideals taught, an American school which
> has failed to be first an instrument of democracy
> has failed fundamentally. In a theocracy such
> schools would be appropriate; in a democracy
> they are an anomaly. It is a sad commentary on
> the trust that religious leaders have in the
> holding power of their own beliefs that they
> dare not spare their young believers five
> hours a day, for five days in the week, for
> nine months in the year, to a training for
> citizenship in company with the varied groups
> which go to the making of an American community,
> lest they lose the faith of their fathers.

In reply to the argument by parochial school advocates of

the inseparability of religious and intellectual training,

Cannon argued:

> In so far as they say that moral and intellectual
> training are inseparable, they speak as Americans.
> When, however, they assert that sectarian and
> intellectual education must take place together,
> they are aligning themselves against what we
> believe to be a principle on which this country
> was founded--fundamental separation between
> Church and State. The danger to the advocates
> of sectarian education is as great as the danger
> to the country as a whole; for the training of
> sectarian groups to think and act as groups means
> the emergence of religious prejudices and intol-
> erance. The greater fellowship is sacrificed to
> the lesser, and these citizens of an America
> which was able to be a refuge for the oppressed
> of all nations are insidiously undermining the
> very foundations of their own security.

Cannon also criticized private schooling based on "social

exclusiveness" for hardening class divisions in society

and preventing the social integration necessary for Ameri-

canization and the development of leadership. Finally, pri-

vate schools based on "intellectual exclusiveness" in their

concern for educational fads and enthusiasms tended to ignore

the most fundamental goal of education in a democracy:

social cooperation and democratic living. Cannon concluded

from this analysis that "interest in the schools founded in

the spirit of exclusiveness and detachment" distracted

necessary attention from "schools founded in the spirit of

democracy." While disapproving of legislative attempts

to abolish private schools, she nevertheless questioned

whether "the time may come when, in sheer self-defense,

a democracy will have to resort to so undesirable an expedient."[37]

---

[37]_Atlantic Monthly_, November 1923 , pp. 611-22, _passim_.

In contrast with this assessment, James H. Ryan in "The Proposed Monopoly in Education" defended the legitimacy and value of private initiatives in education. While equally concerned about the most appropriate form of education for life in a democracy, Ryan challenged an exclusively social understanding of education, emphasizing the principle of idividualism underlying democracy.

> Now a true democracy seeks, as its primary ob-
> jective, the education of the individual, first
> and foremost for his own welfare and for the
> development of his inherent powers and facul-
> ties, and secondly, for the welfare of the
> body social.

Otherwise, the state "becomes . . . tyrannical, an oppressor rather than a protector of individual rights" as in the case of Germany which, under the influence of Hegelian philosophy, "subordinated the individual to the State, the good of Germans to the good of Germany." The results, according to Ryan, were that

> in the mechanical process of making citizens,
> spontaneity, initiative, individual responsi-
> bility, freedom of thought and act become
> completely submerged. The products are
> whole samples of human beings, all modeled
> after the ideal of citizenship which the
> statesman of the hour thinks best.

> Second, Ryan defended the religious basis of democracy.

> It is so essentially a spiritual process that in
> the absence of those moral qualities, like
> self-reliance, self-control, bravery, justice,
> and generosity, which alone make an individual
> upright and strong, it becomes unthinkable.

Because religion and morality constitute "the life blood of democracy, the stuff out of which any lasting democracy must

be fashioned," Ryan argued that there could be no question
that religious education could become "narrowly sectarian"
and "a menace to the maintenance of democratic thought."
Finally, Ryan warned of the dangers of a national system
of schooling portended in Oregon's compulsory public school
law.

> Such laws are so foreign to American ideals,
> so contrary to the past dealings of the State
> as represented by the history of the aid given
> to private educational initiative, so destruc-
> tive of the spirit of fair play and tolerance
> which has always characterized us as a people,
> that it is with chagrin, mixed with fear for
> the future of democracy itself, that we view
> this invasion of a domain always thought of as
> peculiarly free from attacks or interference
> on the part of the state.

If democracy was to survive, education must maintain the
democratic values of "individualism, variety, personal initiative" and "freedom for the individual to work out his
life in the way the individual thinks it must be worked out."
The consequences of such a view demanded from government a
profound respect for the rights of parents in the education
of their children, support of private initiatives in education, and minimal direct involvement in the business of
the schools.[38]

  While the ideological battle lines were clearly drawn
in the public debates over the Oregon school bill, Catholics,
fearful of reinforcing popular fears of Catholic power,
played a low-key role in the initial campaign opposing
passage of the measure, encouraging other opponents to

_____
    [38]"The Proposed Monopoly in Education," Atlantic Monthly,
November 1923, pp. 173-79, passim.

speak out. The Rev. Edwin O'Hara, archdiocesan superintendent of education, was the main public spokesperson for the
Catholic position.[39] Archbishop Alexander Christie of
Oregon City helped to organize the Catholic Truth Society
of Oregon to counter anti-Catholic propaganda disseminated
during the campaign.[40] Although the U.S. hierarchy pledged
their assistance to Archbishop Christie in his efforts,
the National Catholic Welfare Conference was unable to
give any financial aid and, at the time, was "poorly equipped
in defensive literature."[41]

However, this situation was to change after the Oregon
school law won a state-wide referendum by a narrow majority
on 7 November 1922. In January of the following year, the
NCWC administrative committee met with Archbishop Christie
to discuss strategies to win repeal of the Oregon law. The
bishops supported the decision of the NCWC to underwrite
the cost of a judicial appeal process and a nation-wide
campaign of information defending Catholic schools.[42] To

[39]Tyack, "The Perils of Pluralism," p. 86.

[40]Jorgenson, p. 459.

[41]"Important Dates in the History of the Oregon Decision,
Show how the Bishops, through the Administrative Committee,
NCWC Financed and Successfully Prosecuted the Appeal of the
Oregon Anti-Private School Law," NCWC Bulletin 7 (July 1925):11.

[42]"Administrative Bishops of NCWC Hold Important
Meeting," NCWC Bulletin 4 (February 1923):5.

enlist Catholics all over the country in this cause, the
NCWC department of education founded the Catholic School
Defense League whose yearly dues would help to finance
research and dissemination of information supporting the
Catholic position.[43] This led to the publication of the
Catholic School Rights Series, pamphlets detailing Catholic
views on the nature of education in a democracy, objections
to the Oregon school law, and the need for religious education.
James Ryan's Catechism of Catholic Education became one of
the most widely distributed publications from this series.[44]
The education department also coordinated and encouraged
Catholic schools' participation in American Education Week
in another effort "to combat the well-financed and excellently
organized attacks on the Catholic schools." Throughout
the country, Catholic schools and parishes conducted cele-
brations and programs around themes clearly chosen for
their apologetic values: "the Catholic school stands for
authority--the foundation of all government"; "a religious
citizen is the best type of citizen"; "the Catholic parish
school is a distinct contribution to Americanism": and "the
Catholic high school teaches children to be intelligent and
useful Americans."[45] The bureau of education announced a

---

[43]James H. Ryan, "Catholic School Defense League
Explained," NCWC Bulletin 4 (March 1923):27-28.

[44]The Series was advertised in the NCWC Bulletin 4
(February 1923):25.

[45]"American Education Week," NCWC Bulletin 5 (November
1923):30-31.

program of "research work" on the scope of Catholic school-

ing in the U.S. to counter the "constant stream of serious

insinuations and accusations" against the schools.[46]

In all of these efforts, Catholic apologists were

attempting to communicate the fundamental premises under-

lying Catholic schooling in American society. In the words

of A. C. Monahan, director of the NCWC bureau of education,

Catholics were agreed

> that general education for all youths in the
> U.S. is necessary for the well-being of the
> State, and the prosperity, health, and safety
> of its individuals. They agree that it is the
> right and the duty of the State to require
> that all children receive a certain amount of
> education, the minimum being fixed by State
> legislative enactment.
> They believe that the State should main-
> tain free public schools so that this minimum
> education essential to its well-being will
> be available to every child whose education
> is not provided otherwise, and that these
> schools should be supported from public money
> raised by taxation or otherwise from all citi-
> zens regardless of whether or not they have
> children attending public schools. They be-
> lieve that every American citizen should have
> the right to send his child to any type of
> school he may wish provided that the school
> is meeting at least the minimum requirements
> set by the State and that it is truly American
> in its teachings. [Italics in original][47]

In December 1923, the Society of the Sisters of the Holy

Name of Jesus and Mary, who conducted several elementary

Catholic schools in Oregon, and the Hill Military Academy

both filed appeals in the U.S. District Court of Oregon

for an injunction against Governor Pierce and other state

---

[46]Charles N. Lischka "Research Work of the N.C.W.C. Bureau of Education," NCWC Bulletin 5 (April 1924):14-15.

[47]"Work of the NCWC Bureau of Education," NCWC Bulletin 3 (June 1921):18.

officials to prevent enactment of the compulsory public
school attendance law scheduled to take effect in September
1926. Attorney John P. Kavanaugh representing the Society
of Sisters argued that Oregon's school law if enacted would
interfere with the rights of parents to determine the education of their children, deprive teachers of the right
to teach in private schools, violate the charter issued
by the state giving the sisters the right to conduct schools,
deprive the sisters of property without due process, and
interfere with freedom of conscience and religious expression.[48]

In addition to these specific legal points, the hear-
ings also addressed the broader social questions concerning
the limits and responsibilities of government in education
that had been the main focus of public debate. Attorneys
for Governor Pierce argued that the state clearly had the
right to compel children to be educated. Oregon's public
school attendance law, an initiative approved by the majority
of citizens, was simply a means to insure that proper educational standards and social cohesion were maintained, the
accomplishment of these goals justifying the element of
compulsion mandated by the law.

> The great danger overshadowing all others which
> confront the American people is the danger of
> class hatred. History will demonstrate the
> fact that it is the rock upon which many a
> republic has been broken and I don't know any
> better way to fortify the next generation against
> that insidious poison than to require that the
> poor and the rich, the people of all classes
> and distinction, and of all different religious

---

[48]Jorgenson, p. 461.

> beliefs, shall meet in the common schools,
> which are the great American melting pot,
> there to become . . . the typical American
> of the future.[49]

Pierce's attorneys freely admitted that the intent of the law was to destroy the nonpublic schools in Oregon, arguing that such action was warranted because of the dangers to the state from such schools in the increase of juvenile delinquincy, the spread of un-American doctrines, and the eventual destruction of the public school system.[50]

Kavanaugh replied that the issue in dispute was not the state's right to compel school attendance or to set minimum standards in the conduct of public and private schools. In seeking to eliminate private elementary education, the defendants had failed to prove either the inefficiency of private schools or that they constituted a real and direct threat to the state or the common welfare. Another attorney for the sisters disparaged the defendants' claim that public schools healed class divisions; rather the school law merely fostered class hatred by denying parents constitutional rights they had always exercised.[51]

The federal court on 31 March 1924 found in favor of the plaintiffs and issued an injunction against the Oregon school law. The court ruled that Oregon's law constituted

---

[49]Tyack, "The Perils of Pluralism," p. 93.

[50]Jorgenson, p. 462.

[51]Tyack, "The Perils of Pluralism," pp. 93-94.

an arbitrary and despotic exercise of the police powers of
the state because the defendants had failed to show any
compelling need for violating the plaintiff's constitutional
rights and depriving them of property without due process
of law. The court rejected arguments based on the role of
the public school as a melting pot. Citing the U.S. Supreme
Court's decision in the Meyers case which ruled as uncon-
stitutional a law forbidding the use of foreign languages
in Nebraska schools, the court concluded:

> The desire of the legislature to foster a
> homogeneous people with American ideals
> prepared readily to understand current dis-
> cussions of civic matters is easy to appre-
> ciate . . . . But the means adopted, we
> think, exceed the limitations upon the power
> of the state and conflict with rights assured
> to plaintiff.[52]

On 1 June 1925, the U.S. Supreme Court validated the
lower court's ruling in favor of the Society of Sisters
against the Governor. In what has since been hailed as
a Magna Carta for U.S. Catholic schools, the Court upheld
the rights of parents to choose the proper education for
their children.

> The fundamental theory of liberty upon which
> all governments in this Union repose excludes
> any general power of the state to standardize
> its children by forcing them to accept instruc-
> tion from public teachers only. The child is
> not the mere creature of the state; those who
> nurture him and direct his destiny have the
> right, coupled with the high duty, to recog-
> nize and prepare him for additional obligations.

---

[52]Ibid., p. 95.

However, the Court qualified its position by maintaining that nothing in its ruling was to be interpreted as in any way denying

> the power of the state reasonably to regulate
> all schools, to inspect, supervise, and examine
> them, their teachers and pupils; to require
> that all children of proper age attend some
> school, that teachers shall be of good moral
> character and patriotic disposition, that cer-
> tain studies plainly essential to good citizen-
> ship must be taught, and that nothing be
> taught which is manifestly inimical to the
> public welfare.[53]

While the Pierce decision secured the survival of Catholic schools in the United States, it also served to sanction the movement toward making private schools more accountable to public educational standards. Even more fundamentally, it established what one Catholic analyst of the decision called the "beginning of a new era in the relations of the state towards education." With regard to the fundamental political issue of balancing the needs of the state and society against the rights and liberties of the individual, the Court ruled that educational pluralism was not a sufficient threat to the common welfare to justify compulsory methods and serious abridgement of individual freedom. Catholics also inter-preted the Court's decision as a repudiation of "the secularist tendency in American education" which

> has been to separate citizenship from religious
> sanctions, to overemphasize our duties towards

---

[53]"Pierce v. Society of Sisters," in The Supreme Court and Education, ed. David Fellman (New York: Teachers College, Columbia University, 1960), p. 2.

humanity, and to minimize our duties towards
God. The kingdom of earth, not the kingdom
of heaven, has been the exclusive aim of such
educational purposing. The Supreme Court
recalls the country to the original American
standards, wherein since the days of Washington
was recognized the intimate dependence of education on morality, and the fact that the prosperity of all derives from a widespread acceptance
of such a sound attitude towards public education.[54]

The Costs of Institutional Independence

Though Catholic efforts opposing federalization and
the threat of state monopoly were effective in warding off
direct interference in the operation and control of Catholic
schools in the 1920's, that independence was purchased at
some cost. To prove that educational separatism posed no
threat to the larger community, Catholic school leaders
were eager to demonstrate that Catholic schools met the
same high educational standards as public schools. The
NCWC in 1921 took the following position regarding the
proliferation of state laws directly affecting Catholic
schools:

The general trend of educational legislation
is toward standardizing private schools on
the same basis as public schools now function,
both materially and formally, in regard to
qualification of teachers, courses of study,
duration of term, and language of instruction.
These things are not objected to. Catholics
do not fear for their teachers, since they
consider them fit to be certified, with reasonable time allowances given. Courses of study
have been fundamentally the same in public and
private schools. Where they are not, they

---

[54]James H. Ryan, "What the Oregon Decision Means for
American Education," NCWC Bulletin 7 (July 1925):9-10.

ought to be so, for the sake of uniformity,
if for no other reason. Catholics will also
agree that if we are to have a homogeneous
and united nation every principle of citizenship and patriotism demands that the.English
language be the basic language of instruction
in all elementary schools.[55]

The arguments in the brief for the Society of Sisters appeal-

ing Oregon's school law never challenged the state's right

to regulate and supervise private schools, and after the

Supreme Court decision, Catholics' public position remained

the same.

> The Catholic school has no fear of reason-
> able supervision on the part of the state. In
> almost every case it would be welcome. Our
> teachers are so well prepared, our teaching
> is so well done, and our equipment is of such
> a high grade that nothing but good could result
> from the approving inspection of state officials.
> Catholic educators have not slept during the
> last twenty-five years. They are prepared and
> even anxious to meet all the just demands of the
> state, knowing as they do the strong points of
> our system.[56]

For some educators, accepting state supervision was

simply the lesser of two evils and a necessary compromise

to avoid more serious legal restrictions, as, for example,

in the case of Nebraska's Burney Bill in 1919.[57] Others

continued to question the wisdom of a policy of accommoda-

tion with the state, stressing the potential damage to the

integrity and full implementation of Catholic educational

principles. However, most school leaders in the 1920's

---

[55]Lischka, "State Laws Affecting Parochial Schools," p. 21.

[56]Ryan, "What the Oregon Decision Means," p. 10.

[57]See Nepper, "School Legislation in Nebraska," p. 269-70.

felt secure in the Catholic character of the schools; they
felt considerable pressure to demonstrate that they were
also American and equivalent to the public schools. Consequently, the main priority guiding educational practice
in the 1920's was to keep up with rapidly rising public
standards in the conduct of Catholic schools.

Chapter   V

CATHOLIC SCHOOLS AND PUBLIC STANDARDS

The question of Catholic school accreditation or standardization became significant in the 1920's as part of the larger concern of Catholics to defend the integrity and legitimacy of their schools in American society. In response to hostile critics' charges that Catholic schools were un-American and inferior to the public schools, Catholics argued that their schools provided quality education built upon the solid foundation of religion and morality and they embodied, even more faithfully than secular, public schools, the democratic educational ideal envisioned by the founders of the Republic.

But while clearly asserting the civic role of Catholic schooling, the church also insisted on its right to conduct schools free of government interference and fought strenuously against legislation that threatened the independence of Catholic schools. This was a difficult position to defend, and many were in search of a concrete way of demonstrating to the public that Catholic schools took seriously their civic and educational responsibilities without relinquishing crucial institutional control or compromising the integrity of the schools. It is in this context that Catholic educators began to consider a response to the movement toward educational "standardization" as it was called in the 1920's.

Standardization was a movement by state legislatures and voluntary educational associations to formulate and enforce consistent and uniform standards in the conduct of schools, especially high schools. Supported by the progressive fervor for educational reform, organizational efficiency and social control, efforts to establish educational standards touched upon almost all aspects of schooling---pupil attendance, teacher qualifications, curriculum and course requirements, the physical plant and equipment of schools, administration and supervision.

Standardization took two forms. In one case, state legislatures established legal requirements for the conduct of schools, both public and private. Catholic schools had no choice but to meet these minimum legal standards if they wished to continue operating as a publically acceptable alternative to the public schools. By the 1920's Catholic schools were subject to state laws and regulations in regard to the general curriculum, teaching of special subjects, qualifications of teachers, required reports, medical inspection, oaths of allegiance and the supervision and inspection of schools for purposes of compulsory education.[1] Another form of standardization was through a process by which schools voluntarily submitted to evaluation by either the state, through its department of education

---

[1] O'Dowd, p. 5. ('Dowd states that laws applicable to private high schools were indefinite and included few provisions for enforcement.

or state university, or a regional educational association.
Schools meeting standard requirements and regulations become "approved" or "accredited" by that state or regional
agency.

The need for some process of accrediting high schools
arose in the late nineteenth century when the growth of
public high schools had created a problem of articulation
between secondary and college education. In its early
years, "the people's college" was not directed toward preparing its students for college entrance, but as more
students went on for higher education, critics complained
that high schools failed to prepare students to pass entrance examinations to gain admission.

One of the earliest attempts to facilitate the movement from high schools into colleges was a certificate
system created at the University of Michigan. In 1869,
the University began accepting graduates from high schools
previously approved by the University faculty without having to take entrance examinations. By 1895 the system
had spread to other state universities and departments
of education throughout the country, especially in the
mid-west. As high schools became subject to the inspection and approval of any number of universities, the need
for coordination of the accreditation process gave rise
to the formation of regional agencies to supplement the
work of state systems.[2]

See Edward A. Krug, "The Rise of Accreditation" in
The Shaping of the American High School (Madison, Milwaukee,
and London: University of Wisconsin Press, 1969), pp. 146-68.

Prior to World War I, Catholics participated only to a limited extent in this system of accreditation. The first Catholic high schools to gain state accreditation were in California in 1888 and Wisconsin in 1893. Catholics participated in the Middle States Association from its founding in 1887. The North Central Association accredited its first Catholic high school in 1908; the Southern Association in 1913; and the Northwest Association in 1930.[3] The total number of accredited Catholic high schools, however, remained small. For example, by 1915 only a few Catholic high schools were listed among those approved by the North Central Association, the agency that had perhaps the greatest influence on Catholic schools.[4]

Accreditation was not a significant issue for Catholics before the turn of the century. Having only recently committed themselves to the development of a system of parochial schools, Catholic energy and resources in the late nineteenth century were focused on maintaining and expanding elementary education. Though they did offer secondary education through private academies and college preparatory schools in the aristocratic tradition of education for the elite, Catholics lagged behind the larger public in accepting the ideal of universal education on the secondary level. The pressures of high school expansion

---

[3]O'Dowd, pp. 20-25.

[4]Sister Bertrande Meyers, The Education of Sisters (New York: Sheed & Ward, 1941), p. 20.

that had made the problems of the scope, organization,
purposes and functions of high schools such a pressing
concern for the public were yet to be felt in the Catholic
community.[5]

When Catholics became more involved in secondary
education in the 1900's, they were still deeply influenced
by Rome's resolution of the Americanization controversy and
its condemnation of the modernism and continued to be ex-
remely cautious about even the appearance of cooperation with the state. Peter Yorke at the 1912 meeting of
the CEA expressed the typically negative attitude of
Catholics toward any external involvement in Catholic
school affairs.

> This, then . . . I conceive to be the practi-
> cal attitude demanded of the State, namely,
> to continue as we have begun in the strengthen-
> ing and extending of our own system of educa-
> tion in accordance with our own principles and
> ideals. Parish school, and college, and uni-
> versity--let them be our concrete protest
> against secularism and State omnipotence. Those
> who are outside may choose to feast of the flesh-
> pots in the land of bondage, but, as for us and
> our house, we will serve the Lord through whom
> kings reign and princes decree justice.[6]

It was this separatist mentality that led both the Catholic
University of America and the Catholic Educational Association to attempt to establish procedures for the accreditation

---

[5]Burns, Growth and Development of the Catholic School
System, p. 364.

[6]"The Family, the State, and the School," CEA Bulletin
9 (November 1912):86.

of Catholic high schools independent of state and regional
educational agencies operating in the public sphere.

Catholic University's Program of Affiliation

The rapid but unsystematic growth of Catholic high
schools in the first two decades of the twentieth century
focused Catholic educators' attention on the need for organized and coordinated efforts to raise educational standards.
The 1911 meeting of the Catholic Educational Association
was devoted to a discussion of high school standardization.
Of particular concern was a trend reported by James A. Burns
for Catholic high schools to seek accreditation from non-
Catholic institutions. Burns found that of the 295 high
schools he surveyed, fifty-six were accredited or affiliated
with non-Catholic institutions while only nineteen had
sought Catholic accreditation. Burns warned that if this
trend continued, Catholic schools would be in danger of
becoming modeled on public schools. Furthermore, he
claimed that non-Catholic affiliation threatened the
development of a complete system of Catholic schooling
by easing the way for Catholic high school graduates to
attend secular colleges and universities.[7]

Response to Burn's report was divided. Dr. Edward
Pace from Catholic University questioned whether standardization by non-Catholic agencies was compromising the unique

[7]"Report of the Committee on High Schools," CEA
Bulletin 8 (November 1911):54-57.

spirit of Catholic education.[8] James F. Green, president of St. Rita College in Chicago,went even further than
Pace in denouncing the practice as a "heterodoxical spectacle"
and "a stultification of our claim of the necessity of
Catholic education."[9] Bishop Schrembs of Toledo and
Archbishop Messmer of Milwaukee defended the practice, insisting that accreditation simply meant "recognition" and
did not violate the fundamental integrity of the Catholic
school. They allowed non-Catholic affiliation in their
dioceses because they had found it necessary to convince
parents to keep their children in Catholic schools.[10]

With the CEA, Catholic University of America was
also concerned about the challenges that the standardization movement posed to Catholic education in the U.S.
Thomas Shields and Edward Pace in their appeal for the
establishment of a Sisters College at Catholic University
in 1909 had brought the matter to the attention of the
rector, Thomas J. Shahan. Bemoaning "the fact that
Catholic schools are turning to non-Catholic sources for
their ideals and for their standards," Shields and Pace
argued that

> the logical conclusion from this . . .
> is that since the public school system
> is the end towards which our schools

---

[8]"Discussion," CEA Proceedings 8 (1911);67.

[9]"Catholic Education Above the Grammar Grades,"
CEA Bulletin 8 (November 1911):171.

[10]"Discussion," CEA Bulletin 8 (November 1911):183-187.

> shape their courses, the sooner the child
> enters the public school system the better.
> It amounts to a public confession of the
> inferiority of our schools.[11]

The failure of any consensus to emerge at the 1911 CEA
meeting on the issue of standardization convinced Shields
and Pace that any action to establish independent accreditation procedures would have to be initiated by Catholic
University. A plan for the affiliation of Catholic high
schools and colleges proposed by Shields and Pace received
formal approval from the University Board of Trustees in
April, 1912. By setting standards of operation for Catholic
schools, the aim of the affiliation program was

> to bring about unity, harmony, and academic
> excellence within a truly national system
> of education that was thoroughly Catholic
> in character.[12]

The task of encouraging Catholic high schools to participate in the affiliation program fell largely to Shields
who provided much of the leadership of the program till
his death in 1921. When the plan was announced in the
Catholic Education Review, Shields emphasized the benefits
of improved curriculum, teacher training and examination
procedures to participating high schools. Recognizing
that the traditional independence of religious orders
was an obstacle to affiliation, Shields assured his readers
that

---

[11]Quoted in Watrin, p. 40.

[12]Ibid., p. 61.

> what the University aims at is not to lessen
> the autonomy of any institution but rather to
> secure that autonomy in the right direction,
> i.e., to make our schools independent of
> numerous influences which would tie them down
> to a system and method which leave no room for
> the genuine Catholic spirit.[13]

These arguments were persuasive to an increasing number of Catholic high schools and affiliation to Catholic University went from thirty-three high schools in 1912 to a peak of 229 in 1927-28. By 1938-39 the number of affiliated high schools had dropped to 107 and the program was reorganized so that its purpose was no longer standardization or accreditation of Catholic schools. Instead, its goal was simply to provide educational services to promote the development of affiliated schools as Catholic institutions.[14]

Even at its peak, the affilitation program of Catholic University involved only a fraction of the total number of Catholic high schools in the United States. Despite the frequent exhortations of school leaders, the need for institutional independence in the earlier years of the twentieth century, the affiliation program failed dismally as an alternative to state or regional accreditation. By 1920, it had become clear to many that Catholic educational isolation was beginning to break down. Educators began to publicly express views that indicated a far less resolute

---

[13]Ibid., p. 51.

[14]Ibid., p. 211, 185.

opposition to cooperation with non-Catholic educational
agencies, and the practice of Catholic schools seeking
accreditation from non-Catholic sources continued unabated.

The Catholic Educational Association: An Accrediting Agency?

The Department of Colleges and Secondary Schools of
the CEA in 1920 appointed a committee to look into the problems of high school standardization in response to an appeal
by Walter C. Tredtin, principal of West Philadelphia High
School, urging the need for some form of standardization
procedures for Catholic schooling.

> Every high school will welcome standardization
> because once the seal of approbation has been
> impressed upon a school it will accomplish its
> mission with a light heart and with faith in its
> powers of doing efficient work. It is depress-
> ing and discouraging to be groping in the dark-
> ness of uncertainty. The pupils attending the
> high school will have more confidence in their
> school when they know that its work is approved
> by the standardization agency and the public too
> will hold it in more regard and esteem when it
> is assured that the school has measured up to
> the standard.[15]

Underlying this appeal was a general concern about low enrollments and hesitant support for Catholic high schools.
In 1920 the majority of Catholics were yet to be convinced
of the need or the value of such institutions. With college
entrance increasingly dependent on graduation from an
accredited high school, school leaders feared that lacking

---

[15]"The Standardization of Catholic High Schools,"
CEA Bulletin 17 (November 1920):81.

accreditation, Catholic high schools would be at a dis-
advantage in attracting and holding students, particularly
those who were college-bound.

Two separate matters were at issue as the CEA dis-
cussed the question of high school standardization in the
1920's. The first was the desireability of any type of
centralized supervision and evaluation of individual
Catholic high schools. Consistent with the church's position on the importance of local control of education and
the dangers of federal involvement in education, a few
Catholics argued that standardization violated basic Catholic
educational principles. The majority of Catholics insisted
that the times demanded unified and coordinated action if
the schools were to maintain consistent standards of ex-
cellence. The second issue was whether to continue the
practice of actively seeking state accreditation of Catholic
high schools or to attempt once again to establish some
form of internal accrediting through the CEA. The report
of the Committee on Standardization of Catholic High Schools
at the 1921 CEA meetings indicates that these questions
were yet to be fully resolved.

To make some assessment about the need for improving
standards, the Committee had collected data from 186 of the
400 Catholic high schools in the U.S. Assessing the conditions under which these schools were operating against a
provisional set of nine standards, the Committee's findings

were less than desireable: twenty-four schools met all or
all but one of the standards, fifty-seven schools failed
to meet two or three standards, seventy-seven were deficient
in three or four standards, and sixteen failed to meet
between six and all nine standards. The committee made
no explicit judgment about what these figures revealed
about the over-all quality of Catholic high schools or the
need for some type of accrediting process. Members felt
that their task was simply to gather data upon which further
discussions might be based. However, they did focus the
main issue to be decided:

> Shall the Catholic Educational Association
> constitute itself a standardizing agency for
> our Catholic high schools with the view of
> ultimately achieving a reciprocal exchange
> of lists of standardized high schools with
> other such accrediting agencies, or shall it
> merely use its influence on its own member
> schools in urging them to become accredited
> to their own regional associations, and per-
> haps in addition afford some medium for exchange
> of opinion and consolidation of influence
> among its members in the various standardizing
> associations to which they now or later will
> belong?

In view of the U.S. Catholic church's historical commitments
to educational separatism and its understanding of the
school primarily as an agency of religious socialization,
even raising the question as to the proper agency for the
supervision and evaluation of the schools was a critical
departure from tradition. No longer was there unequivocal
opposition to consideration of the matter. The committee,
mirroring divisions in the wider Catholic educational community,

found that its members were not "of one mind in even suggesting an answer to this question."[16]

In an address before the general assembly of the CEA
the year after the committee's report, George Johnson, a
former student of Thomas Shields and professor of education
at Catholic University, offered a critical and detailed
examination of the key arguments surrounding the issue of
standardization. He began by recognizing those Catholics
who "plead for individualism in matters educational" and,
on principle, remained opposed to standardization in any
form. Summarizing their arguments, he stated:

> They see in standardization an attempt to trans-
> fer a method from a field of things mechanical
> and routine and non-human, where it is at home,
> to a field where freedom and individual initia-
> tive and differentiation reign rightfully and
> where as a consequence it must always prove
> an alien intruder. They view askance the develop-
> ment of system in things educational. They fail
> to see where the results of modern education
> justify the growing intricacies of the process.
> Business efficiency seems to be usurping the
> role of culture; . . . elaborate methods of
> supervision seem bent on destroying what must
> always be an essential characteristic of true
> education, the personality of the teacher.
> They foresee . . . a condition . . . when schools
> will be so organized and inter-organized that
> they will constitute a great machine, each part
> finely adjusted to the performance of some definite
> function, all working together according to some
> routine formula. . . . And because a machine is
> never stronger than its weakest part, they see
> the whole process toned down to the level of
> least resistance, the low average becoming the
> measure of the exceptional, the minimum obscuring
> the maximum, the means becoming the end and the
> system destroying the individual.[17]

---

[16]Rev. E. A. Mooney, "Standardization of Catholic High
Schools," CEA Bulletin 18 (November 1921):162-63.

[17]"Principles of Standardization," CEA Bulletin 19
(November 1922):82-83.

To these arguments, Johnson countered that the increasing complexity of modern life placed new demands on education to redefine its social role. The state was beginning to exercise its right to require training for effective citizenship. Business, industry and the professions needed increasingly skilled workers. Students faced the necessity of earning a living, and justice required that they be protected from "shoddy educational wares" and not left "to the mercy of uneven opportunity that would result were every institution a law unto itself."[18]

Johnson was willing to admit that there were dangers to be avoided in the standardization process. It might interfere with "individual autonomy" and, as a result, "reduce everything to dead level uniformity and take from the schools the last vestige of personal initiate and human quality." Schools must avoid the temptation to confuse adherence to quantitative standards with imrpovements in the quality of education.

> If teachers mistake the means for the end,
> if they conclude that because the curriculum,
> the hours, the equipment, meet standard re-
> quirements, their responsibility is at an
> end and their function is simply to tend the
> machine, then of course the whole process
> defeats its own purpose.[19]

However, if proper precautions were taken against these possibilities, Johnson felt that there were positive

[18]Ibid., pp. 85-86.

[19]Ibid., p. 87.

benefits to be derived from proper standardization of
Catholic schools. The guarantee that schools were meeting
recognizable standards "will always prove our best defense"
against charges that Catholic schools provide an inferior
quality of education and will "serve to protect our graduates when they present themselves for matriculation in
higher schools."

> They will feel that they have no apology to
> make to any man for the quality of their
> education. This may serve in turn to render
> our young men and women more positive and
> decisive in the part they play in American
> life. We have been too much inclined to
> assume the defensive, to scent persecution
> on every side, thus lending color to the
> charge of sectionalism so often advanced
> against us, to stand to the side as though we
> were not wanted when things were going forward.[20]

Though Johnson supported the idea of school standardization, he had grave misgivings about Catholic schools submitting
to standards they had no role in forming.

> We must bear in mind that the Catholic school
> exists for the purpose of carrying out the
> teaching office of the Church and it does not
> seem fitting to make it a mere adjunct to some
> State university or place it under the domina-
> tion of some secular authority. By subscribing
> to the standards of some outside agency we may
> easily lose by indirection our most cherished
> and necessary liberties. Are any standards
> entirely neutral, capable of application to
> institutions of whatever philosophical complex-
> ion? Is there any necessary relation between
> the standards of an institution and the aims
> for which it stands? May not curricular stan-
> dardization with its necessary weighing of rela-
> tive values, commit us to an educational philos-
> ophy that is alien to our spirit? May it not

---

[20]Ibid., p. 88.

easily happen that the demands of secular
standardizing bodies will gradually push
religious training further and further into
the background with the consequent secularization of our schools?

The only acceptable solution for Johnson was for Catholics
to "forget the accidental differences that naturally exist
among us" and to insure the integrity of Catholic schools
by joining together to formulate independent standards for
the Catholic school system.

Such an arrangement would relieve us of the constant menace of undue interference on the part
of those who are strangers to our ideals and
our conditions. It would save us from following a leadership that we rather mistrust. It
would insure our autonomy and make it possible
for us to develop according to our own spirit.[21]

To progressives, Johnson's caution seemed excessive.
At the same CEA gathering in which Johnson advanced his
proposal, Claude J. Pernin, S.J. from Loyola University in
Chicago sharply criticized "ultraconservatives" in Catholic
education including those

who have resisted every invasion of the field
by outside agencies of standardization as an
impertinent intrusion on their right to be
let alone and who have condemned our acceptance
of their dominance as the selling of our
'birthright for a mess of pottage.'

In defense of greater cooperation with non-Catholic standardizing procedures, Pernin argued: "without the spirit of
progress where would we be today? . . . The dry rot of any
educational system is inertia and routine."[22]

---

[21]Ibid., p. 89.

[22]"Better Teaching," CEA Bulletin 19 (November 1920):50.

Even conservatives who shared Johnson's concern for preserving the integrity of Catholic schools sometimes arrived at different conclusions. Francis P. Donnelly, S.J. from Holy Cross College in 1919, had severely criticized the "false, materialistic, unhistorical" principals underlying various attempts to standardize education. Nevertheless, he concluded:

> Catholic schools cannot be independent entirely of their environment, and if the whole world is going to be standardized and if the lack of standardization means, for the unthinking, inferiority, then Catholic schools cannot and will not permit that their excellence be questioned . . . . If to-day the fashion is to be standardized, let us not remain unstandardized.[23]

Austin G. Schmidt, S.J. from the University of Detroit reached a similar conclusion in 1921.

> I believe that it is to the advantage of Catholic schools to standardize after the fashion that now prevails. Why waste breath bidding the tides to stand still? Why live in a realm of Utopian dreams and neglect realities? The country desires a certain kind of standardization, and one must have suicidal tendencies if he refuse it.[24]

Johnson's proposal to establish independent standardization procedures for Catholic schools was never acted upon by the CEA, perhaps because of the same division of opinion that had blocked action when the CEA originally considered the issue in 1911. At the 1923 CEA meeting,

---

[23]"The Principles of Standardization," CEA Bulletin 16 (November 1919):139.

[24]"The Philosophy of Standardization," CEA Bulletin 18 (November 1921):83.

the Committee on Standardization of Catholic High Schools
"had been overlooked" in arranging the program for the
secondary section and the delegates decided to refer the
matter to an advisory committee and to postpone any action
until the following year.[25] At that time, the advisory
committee simply reported that "the time was not ripe for
the standardization of secondary schools."[26] That decision ended any further consideration of the establishment
of a separate system for the accrediting of Catholic high
schools in the United States.

State and Regional Accreditation of Catholic High Schools

The decision of the CEA in 1924 established no definite
policy with regard to high school accreditation. No formal
recommendations were made in regard to the value of "standardization" or the wisdom of seeking accreditation from
state or regional agencies. Schools were left free to
judge the matter for themselves and to act accordingly.
However, the inability of both Catholic University and
the Catholic Educational Association to muster support
for a Catholic accreditation system indicates that for
the majority of Catholic school leaders, state recognition
of Catholic schools was a necessary accommodation.

---

[25]"Proceedings," CEA Bulletin 20 (November 1923):153.

[26]"Proceedings," CEA Bulletin 21 (November 1924):200.

In 1927 one educational researcher observed that the

> progress of standardizing certain types of
> Catholic schools by outside agencies has
> already proceeded so far that it is well
> nigh hopeless to attempt to counteract it.[27]

Data on Catholic high school accreditation seem to indicate

that his predictions were accurate. Despite the warnings

of Johnson and others in the early twenties, 48 percent

of all Catholic high schools were accredited by a state

or regional agency in 1926.[28] By 1934, the figure had

risen to 66.4 percent.[29] In assessing the impact of this

trend in 1936, James T. O'Dowd concluded that the

> relationship to the accrediting agencies
> has led the Catholic high school to imitate
> the methods, practices, and organization of
> the public high school.

He found that state and regional accrediting agencies had

affected three broad areas of Catholic school life: general

equipment, teaching personnel, and administration and super-

vision of the schools. Accrediting agencies inspected

schools to insure hygenic conditions, an adequately stocked

library, and appropriate scientific laboratory facilities.

---

[27]Sylvester Schmitz, The Adjustment of Teacher Training to Modern Educational Needs: A Comparative Study of the Professional Preparation of Teachers in the Public and Catholic Elementary and Secondary Schools in the United States, with a Proposed Plan for the Training of Teachers for American Catholic Schools (Atchinson, Kansas: Abbey Student Press, 1927), p. 92.

[28]Directory of Catholic Colleges and Schools (Washington, D.C.: National Catholic Welfare Conference, 1928), p. 252.

[29]O'Dowd, p. 51.

They also set standards for course credits, textbooks,
units of study required for graduation, programs of studies,
class size, teacher and student course loads, length of
class periods and school terms, and the professional and
academic preparation of teachers and principals.[30]

O'Dowd judged that standardization had produced mixed
results in Catholic high schools. On the positive side,
he concluded that

> the influence and pressure exerted by the
> standardizing agencies have done more to
> raise the standards of the Catholic secondary
> school than any action taken within the
> Catholic body itself.

But, on the negative side, as a product of the recommendations and criticisms of state and regional inspectors,

> elements antagonistic to genuine education
> which have worked themselves into the theory
> and practice of the public high school have
> in turn influenced the Catholic high school.
> Theories and practices which lack both scien-
> tific and cultural justification--for example,
> the practical equivalence of extra curricular
> activities and academic subjects with the
> result that educators are losing sight of
> cultural distinctions, the teaching of sub-
> jects which do not require teaching at all,
> an enlarged school program accompanied by no
> home work and a shortened school day, etc.,--
> have found a place in some of the Catholic
> high schools.[31]

[30]Ibid., p. 123, 128-29.

[31]Ibid., p. 122-23.

Had Accommodation Gone Too Far?

O'Dowd's study came at the end of a decade of continuing debate among Catholic educators over the effects of non-Catholic accreditation on Catholic schools. Most Catholics supported the practice with varying degrees of enthusiasm, while others continued to voice strong objections. The president general and former secretary general of the National Catholic Educational Association, Francis W. Howard, was a conservative influence on that organization[32] and repeatedly reminded educators of their duty to preserve the religious character of Catholic schools and to resist "the competition and imitation of secular institutions." Regarding standardization, he reminded the general assembly of the NCEA in 1930 that "in our institution we can determine and maintain a high standard of our own" and cautioned Catholic schools against allowing themselves "to be regulated and governed in affairs of grave importance by the requirements of voluntary educational societies."[33] Henry Woods, S.J., professor of ethics at the University of Santa Clara, went even further to chronicle the abuses standardization had inflicted on Catholic education. A vehement critic of cultural trends, Woods was convinced that standardization

---

[32]This assessment is made by Dr. Ann B. Whitmer and Rt. Rev. Msgr F. G. Hochwalt, "The National Catholic Educational Association: 1903-1951," Catholic School Journal 51 April 1951):128.

[33]"Address of the President General," NCEA Bulletin 27 (November 1930):45.

> works out for all that is worst in the modern
> world, for libertinism of thought, the break-
> ing up of the family, the extirpation of
> Christianity, the demise of God.

Basing his critique on scholastic theology and classical
educational principles, Wood argued, first, that because
secular standards ignored "the Supreme end of man" they
would never serve the cause of true Christian education.

> What is this but to reform man, to destroy
> in him as far as possible the image of God,
> to standardize him according to another
> standard than that established by the Creator
> in the creature.

Second, education whose aim is "to train the youth as to
incline the man to live a life leading to immortal bliss"
must take into account individual personalities and is in-
capable of being reduced to a common set of uniform methods
and practices. Third, standardization invited undue interference of the state in matters over which it has no
authority.

> It is not within the competence of the secular
> power to define for the citizen the education
> he is to receive. State standardization is
> a euphemism for State usurpation . . . .
> That the omnipotent, irresistable State, using
> the citizen for its own purposes, is the term
> of public education today, no one can fail to
> see. That the effect of all our standardizing
> is to rivet the chains, intellectual and moral,
> of such a slavery, is no less evident.[34]

A totally different assessment of the effects of
standardization was offered by Brother Calixtus, F.S.C.,
community supervisor for the Brothers of the Christian
Schools in New York. In contrast with Woods, Calixtus
argued that the Catholic schools have a responsibility not

---

[34]"Standardization and Its Abuses," NCEA Bulletin 25
(November 1928):48-55.

only to the church, but to the state and to present "conditions of life." Though Catholics had resisted legislation
that threatened outside control and bureaucratic interference in education, they had responded more favorably to
voluntary associations because of their "democratic nature."

> We have through these associations invented
> our own way of setting standards and ideals
> . . . there is less danger of throttling the
> spirit of initiative.

As a result,

> the aid given by the various internal standard-
> izing agencies has assisted our Catholic high
> schools very materially in attaining their
> present-day efficiency, so superior in many
> respects to that of yesterday. The material
> equipment, the curriculum, both the quantitive
> and the qualitative phases of the education
> given therein, the training and general equip-
> ment of their teachers, have greatly improved
> during the past twenty years. This healthy ad-
> vancement is due in no small measure to the
> fact that our Catholic high schools have con-
> formed to the standards considered indispensable
> by honest educators.

In addition, Calixtus maintained that student attitudes had
improved as well. Because the quality of their education
is assured, "they feel confident and well prepared to play
a positive and decisive part in American life." He urged
those high schools that remained unaccredited that it was
"imperative" for them to become "listed with the very best
and most progressive standardizing associations."[35]

Bro. Calixtus' assessment for the most part represented the views of two groups particularly responsible

---

[35]"Standardization--What It Shall Do For Our High
Schools," NCEA Bulletin 26 (November 1929):142-43.

for the spread of standardization in Catholic high schools:
religious orders who staffed the high schools, and diocesan
superintendents, who, acting for the bishops, were increasingly responsible for setting educational policy within
a diocese. Both groups in the early twenties became convinced that the survival of Catholic high schools depended
on accreditation and teacher certification and consistently
pursued this policy through the next two decades while
debates about the wisdom of these actions continued.

A course had been set and gradually resistence lessened
as experience with accrediting agencies proved helpful
and generally cordial. As part of his investigation of
the effects of standardization, O'Dowd asked thirty-five
recognized leaders in the field of Catholic secondary education to evaluate the impact of twenty-three standards
and regulations then applicable to accredited high schools
and to rate each item on a scale from "highly beneficial"
to "highly detrimental." Of the twenty-three items, the
educators rated seventeen as highly beneficial or beneficial. Four were judged to have neither positive nor
negative effects. Only two standards--the use of state
approved textbooks in private and parochial schools and
not allowing credit for courses in religion--were rated
as detrimental.[36]

---

[36]O'Dowd, pp. 94-112.

Debates about accreditation by state and regional
agencies were mostly put to rest by 1935. In that year,
the College and University department of the National
Catholic Educational Association adopted the official
position that "the only attitude that the Association can
take toward all the accrediting agencies is one of friendly
cooperation."[37] The softening of opposition to state
accreditation illustrates an evolution in Catholics' understanding of the nature of their educational separatism.
The action of the NCEA signified and formalized Catholics'
belief that accountability to the state was not necessarily
incompatible with accountability to God; their schools,
while remaining fully Catholic, could also be genuinely
public institutions.

---

[37]"Report of the Committee on College Accreditation,"
NCEA Bulletin 32 (November 1935):76.

Chapter VI

THE PROFESSIONALIZATION OF TEACHER EDUCATION

In almost all discussions of the dangers of standardization in the 1920's, Catholic educators concluded that
the surest route to avoid direct state interference in
the schools was to demonstrate Catholics' voluntary adherence to public educational standards. This stance applied
in particular to the issue of teacher certification as
efforts to improve the professional and academic preparation of teachers consumed much of the energy, dedication
and financial resources of Catholic educators during the
twenties.

When the Catholic Educational Association met in
Saint Louis in June, 1919, the main issue of concern was
clearly the trend toward the enlarged activity of the
state in educational matters. A special joint session
had been called bringing together members of the Conference
of Women's Colleges and the provincials of religious orders
to discuss "The State Certification of Teachers in Parish
Grade and High Schools." The women gathered for this occa-
sion bore heavy responsibility for the preparation of the
vast majority of the teaching personnel of the entire
Catholic school system in the United States.[1] In his

_____

[1]By 1920, the overwhelming majority of teachers in the
Catholic schools were religious women. Of 7,324 high school
teachers, 5,065 were religious women, 1,576 were religious
men, 1,576 were lay persons, and 139 were diocesan clergy.
Of a total of 41,581 high school teachers, 30,192 were religious

opening remarks, chairman James H. Ryan emphasized the gravity

of the situation Catholic schools were facing and the need

for coordinated action.

> Each year the State is assuming more and more
> control of the schools, both public and pri-
> vate . . . . The State universities are
> reaching out farther and farther every year.
> The State Boards of Education are almost in
> absolute control of the educational situation
> . . . . If the facts are such, is it not time
> to face them manfully and to prepare ourselves
> to meet the demands which such supervision
> will exact of us?[2]

The conference program consisted of reports by repre-

sentatives of five religious orders with colleges belonging

to the North Central Association of Colleges which identified

state regulations affecting the licensing of teachers in

the mid-west, the response of religious orders to such

requirements, and a proposal for future action. The reports

indicated unanimity among the religious orders on three

basic points. First, although only Nebraska and Indiana had

passed specific legal requirements for the certification

of teachers in private schools, the sisters reported that

religious orders in their respective states all anticipated

---

women, 2,989 were lay persons, 779 were religious men, and
9 were diocesan clergy. Directory of Catholic Colleges and
Schools (Washington, D.C.: National Catholic Welfare Council
Bureau of Education, 1921), p. 962.

[2]"Conference of Women's College," CEA Bulletin 16
(November 1919):213. By 1920, all but six states had estab-
lished state boards of education. See Henry E. Schrammel,
The Organization of State Departments of Education, Ohio
State University Monograph, no. 6 (Columbus: Ohio State
University Press, 1926), p. 5.

some degree of state regulation in the near future. Second,
religious orders assumed the need for state accreditation
of their schools and were determined to meet any obligation such accreditation might demand in the training and
preparation of religious teachers. Finally, all agreed
that the process of obtaining certification of religious
teachers presented major difficulties for religious orders.

One dean indicated that the lack of uniform standards
among the states made it difficult for religious communities
to design appropriate teacher education programs.[3] Another
criticized the common practice of teachers earning credits
through summer school courses, insisting that the process
of obtaining degrees and state certificates needed "speeding
up."[4] Sister Thomas Aquinas from Saint Clara College in
Wisconsin warned that the pursuit of professional studies
to meet legal requirements might interfere with the spiritual
formation of sisters and endanger the Catholicity of the
schools.[5]

Despite these obstacles, all the reports acknowledged
the need for more thorough professional education for
teachers, especially considering the poor state of teacher
preparation under which religious communities then operated.

---

[3]Sister Antonia, "Interstate Certification of Teachers,"
CEA Bulletin 16 (November 1919):217.

[4]Sister Mary Antonia, "The Certification of Teachers
in Iowa and Nebraska," CEA Bulletin 16 (November 1919):224.

[5]"Certification of Teachers in the Catholic Schools of
Wisconsin," CEA Bulletin 16 (November 1919):232.

Reporting the results of her survey of one third of Catholic
school teachers in Wisconsin, Sister Aquinas found that
while 37 percent of these teachers had some college training, fully 59 percent had less than four full years of
high school education.[6] Such figures were by no means
unusual in other areas of the country at the time and,
given the trend toward increasing state minimum requirements
for the certification of teachers, offered convincing evidence that something needed to be done.

As a result of their discussions, the joint conference
adopted a plan proposed by Dr. Mary A. Molloy, dean of
the College of St. Teresa, "whereby the certification of
teachers might be more efficiently and more quickly secured."
The plan called for each religious order having a college
approved by the North Central Association of Colleges to
open a normal school that would be fully endorsed by the
state to issue teaching certificates in the same manner
as the state's normal schools. Religious orders who did
not operate colleges were urged to organize six week summer
sessions and to invite the state department of education
to conduct certificate examinations. If this were not
possible, religious orders were advised to allow their
sisters to attend the normal schools operated by other
religious communities.[7]

---

[6]Ibid., p. 230.

[7]"Conference of Women's College," p. 215.

The decision of this conference to recommend state certification of religious teachers was part of a widespread consensus among Catholic educational leaders on the need to pursue such a policy. Superintendents of education were becoming increasingly central in the 1920's in exercising responsibility for the coordination and unification of Catholic educational policy and practices on a diocesan level. At their assembly at the 1919 CEA convention, state certification was a major issue on the agenda. After reviewing and comparing trends of state legislation in various parts of the country, the superintendents agreed as a body

> to prevail on the superiors of the different
> teaching communities to take adequate measures
> to provide all teachers with certificates,
> either issued or acknowledged by the State.

Further, they agreed that "to delay action till the law compels such certification is not prudent."[8]

The newly organized Bureau of Education of the National Catholic Welfare Council also indicated support of a policy of state certification of Catholic teachers. In one of its first publications, "Laws and Regulations Relative to Certification of Teachers" published in 1921, the NCWC took the position that raising the standards of the professional education of Catholic teachers was the most important defense that Catholic schools had against further encroachments

---

[8]"Superintendents' Section," CEA Bulletin 16 (November 1919):320.

of the state into private education.[9]   Later, religious

superiors were to report that pastors in charge of parochial

schools had often encouraged teaching sisters to obtain

state certification in hopes of making their schools more

acceptable to obtain state aid.[10]

Despite agreement that state certification of teachers

was a necessary expedient, some Catholics expressed grave

reservations about a policy that seemed inconsistent with

the Church's traditional understanding of the limits of

the state's authority in education. Paul L. Blakely,

associate editor of the Jesuit weekly, America, was an out-

spoken critic of even minimal cooperation with the growing

role of the state in education. Blakely saw the trend in

education in the 1920's as tantamount to the establishment

of

> the Hegelianized Federal Superstate, upon which
> will be built in turn Federalized control of
> the educational, financial, health and religious
> interests of the people.

In theory, Blakely argued, "it is no function of the State

to educate, much less to monopolize education," and, there-

fore, "the State has no right whatever to require the

certification of teachers." But in practice Blakely ad-

mitted that Catholics must recognize that

> the State has no right to do a multitude of
> things which it daily does. But it has the

---

[9]"Certification of Teachers and Legal Requirements
in Various States," NCWC Bulletin 2 (May 1921):20.

[10]Meyers, p. 25.

> power to do them, and that power we cannot
> now profitably resist . . . . In all our
> States to-day, either by custom or by law,
> our parish schools are accredited only on
> condition that the training of their teachers
> and the content of their courses of study are
> substantially those of the State system. In
> other words, whether we approve or not, the
> public school either is or tends to be the
> model to which we conform ourselves.

Blakely urged religious superiors to see that the teaching
sister "be given the fullest opportunity to equip herself
with the professional knowledge upon which to-day depends
her entrance into the classroom" in order that sisters,
traditionally distinguished "in the science of the saints"
may come to "win an honorable place in the science of
the schools."[11]

One of the few voices in these early discussions to
question the assumption that state certification was an
inevitable choice for Catholic teachers was George Johnson,
then superintendent of parish schools in Toledo, Ohio.
While granting the wisdom of some form of certification
process, Johnson urged that Catholics remain cautious about
granting the state the right to pass on the fitness of
Catholic teachers. He conceded there were advantages to
Catholic schools from such a course of action.

> Precedents are adduced from other countries
> to prove that State certification is not
> an unmixed evil, and it has been shown quite
> conclusively that there is nothing in the
> movement contrary to the expressed law of
> the Church. It is pointed out that we can
> meet the arguments of un-Americanism with

---

[11]"The Certification of Teachers," CEA Bulletin 17
(November 1920):450-53.

better grace if our teachers are on the same
footing as the teachers in the public schools.
The difficulties that might come in the way
of obtaining such certificates because of
bigotry and ill-will are minimized, no doubt
rightly. Nor does any State at the present time
maintain standards that should cause us to
worry . . . . And in general the immediate
results might prove very happy for our schools.[12]

But Johnson admitted still "feeling a bit uneasy about the

whole situation," and offered an alternative "that would

standardize teacher training while it precluded State

interference." He proposed that ecclesiastical authori-

ties in each state could establish independent procedures

for granting teaching certificates to Catholic teachers

that would maintain at least all the standards which the

state demanded of its teachers. Since this plan could

insure that Catholic teachers met minimum educational

standards, the state would have no cause for interference.

The plan would also allow the professional training of

religious teachers to continue in their own communities.

Johnson felt that Catholic schools in 1921 were mov-

ing too quickly in the direction of state certification

without sufficient reason.

Because a few States have signified their
intention of certifying religious teachers,
we should not be in too much of a hurry to
commit the whole country to this policy.

As it was, "too many Sisters are being forced by circumstances

to attend State normals and secular universities," because

---

[12]"A Plan of Teacher Certification," CEA Bulletin 18
(November 1921):390.

professional training was often unavailable under Catholic
auspices. Johnson closed his argument with a plea for
caution.

> When all is said and done, it should be the
> aim of the Catholic school system to be as
> self-sufficient as possible, and we should
> be mighty careful of the sacrifices we make
> in the name of opportunism. . . . At least
> let us take our time and not rush blindly
> into an arrangement which may eventually
> nullify the efforts of the Church to provide
> her children in the United States with a re-
> ligious education.[13]

Despite Johnson's consistent plea for internal standardization of Catholic schooling including accreditation and
teacher certification, most Catholic educators agreed with
Ralph L. Hayes, superintendent of parish school of Pittsburgh,
who in response to Johnson's proposal insisted that Catholics
had little choice but to accept state standards.

> We should indeed beware of undue State inter-
> ference . . . . Nevertheless, it is State
> requirements that we have to face, either
> as a fact or as a proximate eventuality.[14]

In reality though, it was not simply the fear of statua-
tory regulation that motivated Catholic teachers to seek
state certification. Given the postwar climate of hostility
toward Catholic schools, Catholic fears that states would
impose legal minimum standards of teacher preparation
were justified but never fully realized. By 1928 only
four states (Alabama, South Dakota, Michigan and Nebraska)

---

[13]Ibid., p. 394.

[14]"The Problem of Teacher Certification," CEA Bulletin
19 (November 1922):367.

had made state teaching certificates mandatory for Catholic
school teachers, while seven others had legislated specific
requirements for the qualifications applying to all teachers
of compulsory school age children.[15] Though the threat of
state imposition of teaching standards was frequently cited
as a key argument supporting a policy of voluntary certification, there was a more immediate and compelling motivation.
Teacher certification was becoming a common means by which
state universities or boards of education evaluated the
qualifications of teachers in granting state accreditation
of high schools. The decision to seek such accreditation
was entirely voluntary and thus involved no legal mandate.
But in seeking accreditation for Catholic high schools,
educators were faced with the necessity of meeting the
state's requirements for the academic and professional
preparation of teachers.[16] Despite a strong plea for independence from state control, Catholics were voluntarily
submitting to the states' educational standards to insure
state approval of their schools.

This accommodation did not go unnoticed. George
Johnson remarked that he found it strange "that our own

[15]See Lischka, Private Schools and State Laws.

[16]Because accreditation applied usually only to high
schools, the increased attention to professional education
focused on high school teachers. There was no similar kind
of external compulsion in the elementary field. See John
R. Hagan, "Catholic Teacher Education," in Essays on Catholic
Education in the United States, ed. Roy J. Deferrari (Washington
D.C.: Catholic University of America Press, 1942).

people would value the seal of another approval rather than our own."[17] In a study of the education of sisters, Sister Bertrand Meyers concluded that

> state affiliation exerted more pressure to
> increase teaching standards than any other
> internal factor. Civil authority commanded
> more respect than Church authority in setting
> standards that were adhered to.[18]

The history of Catholic efforts to improve teacher education prior to 1920 bear out this judgment.

Teacher Education Prior to 1919

In its formal commitment to the creation of a system of separate schools at the 1884 Baltimore Council, the U.S. Bishops also emphasized the importance of maintaining and improving the quality of those schools. To this end, Council legislation established a policy on the certification of Catholic school teachers. Each diocese was to set up a board for the examination of teachers. On passing both oral and written exams, a teacher could receive a temporary certificate valid for five years at which time, a teacher could earn a life certificate by passing a second examination.

When Cardinal Satolli was asked to review this legislation in order to mediate disputes over the proper implementation of the Baltimore decrees, he urged that in addition

---

[17]"The Philosophy of Standardization," p. 89.

[18]Meyers, p. 33.

to obtaining diocesan certification, Catholic teachers
should also seek a diploma from the school board of the
state. He also recommended that normal schools under
Catholic auspices

> should reach such efficiency in preparing
> teachers of letters, arts and sciences,
> that their graduates shall not fail to ob-
> tain the diploma of the State.[19]

Satolli's recommendations, accepted by the hierarchy in 1892,
were based on the conviction that in order to prosper
Catholic schools needed to demonstrate to parents, the
public and state authorities that they were in no way inferior to the public school system.

However, despite official policy, there was little
significant improvement in levels of teacher preparation
prior to 1919. The diocesan examination boards, where
they existed at all, functioned poorly. Often, board
members appointed by the Bishop were not educators and un-
qualified to make judgments about the suitability of appli-
cants for teaching. Many were pastors and administrators
whose primary educational concern was the severe shortage
of teaching personnel for the rapidly expanding school system. Given the enormous demand for teachers, earning a
temporary teaching certificate became "more or less a
formality."[20] By 1920, the whole system of diocesan boards

---

[19] Quoted in John Raphael Hagan, The Diocesan Teachers
College: A Study of its Basic Principles (Washington, D.C.:
Catholic University of America, 1932), p. 15.

[20] Johnson, "A Plan of Teacher Certification," p. 391.

had become "merely perfunctory."[21] At that time, only
seven dioceses in the U.S. had examining boards while only
two diocesan superintendents of schools were able to report they had actually issued teaching certificates.[22]

Standards of teacher education were very low during
this period, even for public school teachers. According
to the U.S. Commissioner of Education, only 18% of public
school teachers in 1884 had two years of normal training.[23]
Among religious orders, the desperate appeals for more
teachers from pastors and the relative poverty of most
communities encouraged a common practice of sending novices
to teaching positions only shortly after joining the order.
Any formal training for teaching was obtained in-service,
either through courses offered in the novitiate or through
an apprenticeship arrangement with an older, more experienced
teacher in the religious community.[24]

The first major shift in this pattern of teacher
education was initiated by the Catholic University of
America in Washington, D.C. beginning around the turn of
the century. As the capstone of the entire Catholic education system in the U.S., the University felt a particular
responsibility to provide direction, guidance and leadership

---

[21]Patrick J. McCormick, "Church Law on the Certification of Catholic Teachers," CER 20 (May 1922):263.

[22]Hagan, The Diocesan Teachers College, p. 14.

[23]Ibid.

[24]Meyers, p. 6.

for Catholic schools, especially through the education
of teachers, supervisors, and administrators. Under the
leadership of Dr. Edward A. Pace in 1902, the University
established an extension center in New York called the
New York School of Pedagogy to offer education courses
to prepare Catholic teachers seeking a New York teachers
certificate.[25] In 1907, Pace and Dr. Thomas E. Shields
convinced the University trustees of the need for a department of education to improve teacher education and coordinate
the development of curriculum, methods and textbooks for
Catholic schools. Because women were excluded from University attendance until 1929-30, the department's early
work focused on the training of priests for positions of
educational leadership.

However, in the summer of 1911, Catholic University
introduced a significant innovation in teacher education
with the establishment of the Catholic Sisters College of
Catholic University under the leadership of Shields. Shield's
original vision was for the University to unify and strengthen
the Catholic school system by becoming the main teacher
training institution for all religious women in the United
States. In addition to providing badly needed professional
education in Shield's view, the Sisters College would help
to break down the relative isolation of religious communities
from one another.

---

[25]In 1904 New York's Archbishop Farley assumed leadership, changing its name to the Institute of Scientific Study.
Watrin, p. 22.

The urgent demand for Catholic schools during
the latter half of the nineteenth century
brought into existence several hundred distinct
communities of teaching Sisters, each of which
tended to remain isolated in its ideals and
methods. This isolated condition was not in
harmony with the genius or the organization of
the Catholic Church, and it offered many obstacles to legitimate progress in the field
of Catholic education. The Council of Baltimore
adopted measures for the organization of the
schools in each diocese, but these were not sufficient to break down the barriers which had
spontaneously grown up around each teaching
community. This isolation was still further
emphasized by the schools developed to take
care of the children of our foreign populations
. . . . The actual accomplishment of this
work (i.e., bringing the separate communities
together) fell largely to the extension work
of the University professors and particularly
to the Catholic Sisters College.[26]

Shield's broad vision for Sisters College never even

approached realization. Although it attracted many religious

to its campus, the expansive aims of Sisters College were

limited by traditional constraints. Religious communities

often could not afford the expense of room, board and tui-

tion needed to educate sisters away from the motherhouse.

Religious superiors tended to see education as a danger

to, or, at best, a distraction from a sister's primary

concern--the spiritual life. Then, too, they feared that

if sisters from different communities were allowed to

study together, this might result in a weakening

of a sister's loyalty to her own community's traditions,

spirit and ideals. As long as the church made no compelling

demands for higher teaching standards, few efforts were

_____

[26]Quoted in Hagan, The Diocesan Teachers College, p. 17.

made to overcome these obstacles and little progress was made in improving the general quality of Catholic teacher education in the United States

The Expansion of Catholic Teacher Education

By 1919 Catholics were generally agreed that state accreditation of schools and certification of teachers was the surest way to fend off criticism of their schools and demonstrate that the education they offered was "in no way inferior" to the secular education offered in the public schools. Discerning the trend among state boards of education to require increasingly higher minimum levels of professional and academic preparation and to rely less on examination procedures in issuing state teaching certificates, educators recognized that past patterns of teacher education would no longer be adequate.[27]

However, in the search for improved means and methods for the education of teachers,

> there was no unanimity of opinion as to how the new demands were to be met, and no definite plan of action outlined; the various Communities were left . . . more or less to their own initiative and resources.[28]

Furthermore, attempts to provide higher education for religious had to contend with the traditional problems that

---

[27]In 1921 only four states required some professional training beyond high school for certifying teachers. By 1930, thirty-one states had such requirements. See Meyers, p. 35.

[28]Ibid., p. 36.

plagued Catholic education. The expansion of Catholic
high schools in the first quarter of the century had ex-
acerbated the shortage of teachers. Few could be allowed
to leave their positions for full-time study. In-service
training remained the rule. Lack of finances and the resistance of religious superiors to secular education outside the community added to the difficulties. Moreover,
there were limited opportunities for higher education for
religious men and women under Catholic auspices. In the
face of such challenges, the twenties became a period of
experimentation and innovation by religious communities,
universities, colleges, and diocesan organizations to
develop new structures to meet the suddenly inflated educational needs of religious teachers.

Initially, religious communities continued to bear
the greatest burden for the education of religious through
community normal schools. In 1924 there were 92 community
normal schools that enrolled 17,067 students, approximately
one-fourth of all Catholic elementary and high school
teachers. By 1930 there were only forty-four such schools
in operation and enrollments had declined by almost half.[29]
This decline indicated, in part, a recognition that many
community normals were simply ill-equipped to offer professional teacher training. In a study of Catholic teacher
training in 1926, Sylvester Schmitz reported on the conditions

[29]Directory of Catholic Colleges and Schools, 1928,
p. 235 and 1932-33, p. 104.

he had observed in his examination of twenty community

normal schools:

> we saw that only a few of the institutions
> have adopted the differentiated curricula
> designed to prepare teachers for different
> types of teaching service, that the consti-
> tuent courses in many institutions are ill-
> adapted to the needs of teachers in the elemen-
> tary schools, that there is no uniformity
> regarding the courses offered, that the librar-
> ies are woefully inadequate, that the practical
> training offered is both insufficient in amount
> and unsatisfactory in the method of administer-
> ing it, and finally that there is a lack of
> proper co-ordination between the theoretical
> and practical training.[30]

In addition to being educationally weak, about half of

these community normals were not accredited and unable to

help students meet state certification requirements.[31] More-

over, by this time normal schools throughout the country

were giving way to teachers colleges as the main agency

for the education of teachers. Individual communities

could not hope to offer comparable levels of professional

training.

To alleviate some of these problems, several dioceses

in the 1920's and 30's established diocesan normal schools

or teachers colleges. Conceived as parallel to the diocesan

seminary for the training of priests, the aim of the diocesan

teachers college was to eliminate the duplication of

---

[30]Schmitz, The Adjustment of Teacher Training, p. 132.

[31]Nine of the twenty community normals surveyed by
Schmitz were accredited by state departments of education.
Nationally, an NCWC survey of 70 normal schools in the
U.S. in 1924 found that 49.2% were accredited. Ibid., p. 78.

educational effort and expense by coordinating all teacher
training within one diocese. Originating in the dioceses
of Brooklyn and Toledo in 1922, the innovation spread
within several years to Witchita, St. Paul, New Orleans,
Cincinnati, and Pittsburg.[32]

Diocesan teachers colleges offered several advantages
over community normal schools. Proponents argued that diocesan
teachers colleges would be more readily recognized by the
state for accreditation purposes and eliminate the need
to send religious to state normal schools. A diocesan
institution could provide a wider range of course offerings
with more qualified instructors far more economically than
could individual communities. Finally, some argued, such
schools might serve to unify and coordinate educational
work by breaking down some of the barriers between religious
communities and encouraging cooperation to solve diocesan-
wide problems.[33]

Despite strong and vocal advocates for diocesan
teachers colleges, religious communities tended to resist

---

[32]See Hagan, The Diocesan Teachers College.
Though similar, these institutions varied considerably with
respect to their organization and structure, financing,
levels of education offered, and relationships with local
colleges and state departments of education. See Schmitz,
"Supervision and Administration of Catholic Teacher Training,"
The Adjustment of Teacher Training, pp. 91-123; William P. A.
Maguire, Catholic Secondary Education in the Diocese of Brooklyn
(Washington D.C.: Catholic University of America, 1932); Richard
J. Bollig, History of Catholic Education in Kansas, 1836-1932
(Washington, D.C.: Catholic University of America, 1933); and
Edward A. Connaughton, A History of Educational Legislation and
Administration in the Archdiocese of Cincinnati (Washington, D.C.:
Catholic University of America Press, 1946).

[33]Hagan, "Catholic Teacher Education." See also Sister
Etheldreda Heard, "A Critical and Constructive Study of the

the idea. In Schmitz's survey of 36 religious communities
in 1926, 53% favored diocesan teachers colleges, while 47%
were opposed.[34] A similar survey in 1938 by Sister
Etheldreda Heard found that acceptance by communities declined significantly as a result of experience with such
colleges: only 16% supported the institution of diocesan
teachers colleges. The studies by Schmitz, Heard, and
Meyers each reported similar objections from religious
communities. One of the most frequently voiced concerns
was that diocesan teachers colleges that provide for the
mingling of religious from different orders threatened
the transmission of a community's unique spirit and educational ideals, especially for younger sisters. One dean
of studies reports:

>   From experience, our Community does not
> favor the diocesan teacher college as a type
> of training for novices. It is not good for
> the particular spirit of vocation; it takes
> the novice away from community life just when
> she needs it most; just as she is about to
> apply the theory of the Novitiate to the daily
> practices of convent life. Each novice needs
> her own environment if she is to grow in the
> spirit of her Order. There will always be
> Sisters, good in themselves, who . . . have
> true vocation, no doubt, but they need to be
> shielded, guided; and one is not always able
> to foresee this until an occasion arises.
>   Such a college is all right for older
> Sisters, imbued with the spirit of vocation;

Organization, Control and Administration of the Teacher-
Training Program for Religious Teachers in Catholic Elemen-
tary Schools" (Ph.D. dissertation, Saint Louis University,
1938), p. 187; Joseph V. X. McClancy, "The Community Normal,"
CER 20 (May 1922):264-273; and Frances J. Macelwane, "A
Plan for the Development of a Diocesan School System,"
CER 22 (February 1924):26-42.

[34]Schmitz, The Adjustment of Teacher Training, p. 108.

> the interchange of thought made possible by
> the mingling of many Communities is broaden-
> ing and invigorating--but it should not come
> too soon in a young Nun's life.[35]

A related fear was that a diocesan institution would come
to be dominated by one particular order to the detriment of
other communities. The time and expense of sending sisters
to a diocesan school located at a distance from the motherhouse was prohibitive to some communities. Finally, diocesan
training was impractical for communities teaching in more
than one diocese where requirements for teacher preparation
often differed.

Another alternative grew out of the desires of religious
orders to preserve some degree of autonomy in the education
of teaching sisters while providing them with the higher
education necessary for state certification. After considering the financial and spiritual costs of sending sisters
away from their communities for education, some orders
decided it would be to their advantage to open their own
colleges. This sentiment led to the establishment of sixty
new Catholic women's colleges in the U.S. between 1920
and 1938.[36] These newer institutions joined older
Catholic colleges and universities in attempting to respond
to the teacher education crisis by creating departments of

---

[35]Quoted in Meyers, pp. 101-102.

[36]Statistics from the Directory of Catholic Colleges
and Schools, 1928 and 1938. Cited by Meyers, p. 44.

education,[37] opening summer schools, and offering extension[38] and correspondence courses.[39]

However, colleges were unable to offer a completely satisfactory solution to the problem of teacher education. Though women's colleges were specifically founded to train Catholic school teachers, continuing teacher shortages prevented sisters from engaging in full-time study. The results, according to one Dean in 1940, was that "since there were more girls than Sisters, our interest centered on girls" and the institution became "just another college for women."[40]

Attendance at Catholic colleges did not necessarily insure that students would remain sheltered from external influences or that programs of teacher education were free of the secular trends that so many found objectionable in

---

[37]See Jane Dominic Birney, O.P., "The Development of Departments of Education in Catholic Universities and Colleges in Chicago, 1910-1960" (Ed. D. dissertation, Loyola University, 1961) and Clarissa M. Doyle, "Teacher Education in Catholic Colleges and Universities of the United States," (Ph.D. dissertation, Fordham University, 1955).

[38]The number of Catholic universities and colleges offering summer courses increased more than 45% between 1921 and 1926. Sylvester Schmitz, "The Trend of Teacher Training," CEA Bulletin 24 (November 1927):346-66. Between 1922 and 1924, institutions offering extension courses increased 43%. Schmitz, The Adjustment of Teacher Training, p. 126.

[39]Francis M. Crowley, "Correspondence Study in Catholic Universities," NCWC Bulletin 5 (December 1923):13.

[40]Meyers, p. 44.

non-Catholic institutions. For example, a study of the
development of departments of education in Catholic universities and colleges in Chicago between 1910 and 1960 by
Jane Dominic Birney found that in all cases,

> the number and variety of the professional
> courses have followed popular trends . . .
> [and] have gravitated closely around the
> demands of local, state, and regional certi-
> fication requirements at the undergraduate
> level. . . . The stipulations of profes-
> sional education requirements [by the North
> Central Association of Colleges and Secondary
> Schools] even in the early 1920's had probably
> the greatest effect upon the preparation of
> secondary school teachers and principals in
> this area until the 1940's.[41]

Chicago offers one example of what was happening to Catholic
institutions across the country. By 1933, all states
exercised close supervision over the teacher training work
of private institutions whose graduates would be qualified
for state teachers certificates. Eight states gave general
power to state universities to set standards binding on
all teacher education programs. Other states enacted
specific legal requirements to be enforced by the state
educational agency. For example, twenty states proscribed
courses of study, seventeen states established graduation
requirements, twelve set admission requirements and credit
hours required in educational subjects, and in eleven states,
the laws specifically required that teacher education in private schools be "equivalent" to that given in state teacher
training institutions.[42]

---

[41]Birney, pp. 206-207; 212.

[42]John H. McNeely, "Supervision Exercised by States Over
Privately Controlled Institutions of Higher Education," Bureau

Other external influences were less direct, but
nonetheless significant. In some cases state or regional
accrediting agencies required colleges and universities
to have on their faculties a certain percentage of professors who had earned their degrees from graduate schools
recognized by the Association of American Universities.
Since Catholic University for a time was the only recognized
Catholic graduate school in the country, Catholic colleges
were often staffed with faculty members who received their
training at non-Catholic institutions. Three religious
provincials in Meyers' study complained that even Catholic
colleges failed to offer "a thoroughly Catholic education."
One provincial explained why she had withdrawn sisters from
a nearby Catholic college:

> We find that where teachers have been trained
> at state universities, they are tainted with
> non-Catholic ideas, and that they give a cast
> to such subjects as Psychology and History as
> occasions us anxiety and even alarm. Our Sisters
> have imbibed ideas of pragmatism which have
> worked havoc with the Catholic spirit, though
> not one has ever attended any but a Catholic
> college.[43]

Indeed, some of the more prominent and influential leaders
in Catholic education in this period were products of secular
graduate training. Dr. Thomas Edward Shields, founder of
Sisters College, professor of education at Catholic University

---

of Education Bulletin, no. 8 (Washington, D.C.: U.S.
Government Printing Office, 1934), pp. 28-29.

[43]Meyers, p. 71.

and editor of the Catholic Education Review, as a young
priest had been sent by Bishop John Ireland to study science
at Johns Hopkins University. His colleague and mentor at
Catholic University, Edward A. Pace, had studied psychology
under Wilhelm Wundt in Leipzig. Dr. Edward A. Fitzpatrick,
author, long-time editor of the Catholic School Journal and
president of Marquette University, had earned his doctorate
from Teachers College, Columbia University during the heyday
of progressive education.

These educational leaders were but a few of the many
Catholic teachers at all levels of Catholic education who,
because of the difficulties or inadequacies of teacher training under Catholic auspices, had chosen to attend state
normal schools or public colleges and universities. In
1926, Schmitz found that fourteen percent of the elementary
teachers and thirteen percent of the high school teachers
he had surveyed had received all or part of their education in secular colleges, state teachers colleges or normal
schools.[44] Despite frequent and vociferous criticisms,
the practice continued to increase between 1920 and 1935 and
diminished somewhat between 1935 and 1940.[45] In 1938,

---

[44]Schmitz, The Adjustment of Teacher Training, pp. 25, 42.

[45]Based on estimates from a sample of religious communities. Figures obtained from 38 non-Catholic institutions
show a steadily decreasing enrollment between 1925 and 1940.
According to these estimates, there were 2,210 sisters enrolled between 1925 and 1930, 1,753 sisters enrolled between
1930 and 1935, and 1,491 sisters enrolled between 1935 and
1940. Meyers, pp. 75-76.

Heard found that ten percent of the 18,370 sisters included
in her study, representing 105 religious communities had
or were attending secular universities.[46]

Only a few of the religious superiors Meyers inter-
viewed actually approved of the practice of sending sisters
to secular institutions. In support of the practice, one
provincial reported:

> On the contrary, it has effected much good.
> A better understanding with secular authori-
> ties exists, and the Sisters themselves are
> broader in outlook. Intellectually, they
> are equal, though not superior, to those
> trained at Catholic schools; but I feel that
> the experience has been good for the Sisters,
> and excellent for those who came in contact
> with them at the State university.[47]

Fifty-seven of the sixty provincials and thirty-seven of
forty-three deans consulted by Meyers opposed the practice,
claiming that it was against the wishes of Rome and set a
bad example for Catholic youth who were constantly admonished
about the dangers of non-Catholic schools. Some felt that
teachers trained at secular colleges "contaminated" the
atmosphere of Catholic schools, offering instruction,
especially in the humanities, that was "naturalistic,"
"persistently paganistic," and "not only out of harmony
but frankly antagonistic to Catholic doctrine."

But in spite of their principled opposition, in
practice, forty-five of the fifty-seven provincials admitted

---

[46]Heard, p. 229.

[47]Meyers, p. 70, 72-73.

that they continued to send sisters to non-Catholic
institutions for teacher training. The persistent demand
from pastors for more and better qualified teachers in
some cases overrode even the strongest reservations about
the appropriateness or desirability of certain kinds of
education for sisters. This situation illustrates the bind
religious orders struggled under as a result of the conflicting impulses shaping Catholic teacher education beginning
in the 1920's.

Impact of Certification Requirements on Catholic Schooling

The advent of school accreditation and teacher certification in the 1920's sent the Catholic community in search
of "a more satisfactory and permanent solution of the teacher
training problem"[48] that would win acceptability for
Catholic schools while preserving the purposes and values
of an older educational tradition. To religious orders in
particular fell the responsibility to work out a practical
course of action that would honor the church's commitments
to school expansion,[49] state certification, and preserving
the spiritual integrity and identity of the religious life
and the Catholic school. But in practice, these three goals

---

[48]Schmitz, The Adjustment of Teacher Training, pp. v.-vi.

[49]The doubling of the number of Catholic high schools
between 1915 and 1925 plus the steady growth of elementary
schools created a critical teacher shortage that coincided
with the demand for better trained teachers.

were often in tension, and despite trying a variety of
approaches, religious communities found themselves forced
to make educational choices that seemed to compromise one
or the other of these obligations.

Thus, the development of Catholic teacher education
in the 1920's produced mixed results that few found entirely
satisfactory. Nevertheless, the period did introduce a
radically new set of expectations and standards as academic
and professional development was added to the traditional
goal of spiritual formation in the education of teaching
sisters. For the first time, religious men and women began
enrolling in some form of higher education. Between 1921
and 1926 the number of students attending Catholic summer
schools increased by over 50% (88.5% were religious women)
and the number of sisters attending summer normal courses
offered by religious communities increased 176%. More than
36,000 teachers, nearly three quarters of the 50,000
teachers staffing Catholic schools were taking summer and
extension courses of various kinds. According to one esti-
mate, these practices enabled Catholic teachers on the
whole to keep pace with the standards operative in the
public system in the twenties. Although his data was
limited, Schmitz calculated that the average length of
preparation for teaching among elementary religious
teachers (1.63 years) was higher than for public elementary
teachers (1.32 years). On the secondary level, Catholic
teachers compared even more favorably with their public

school counterparts. Seventy-five percent of teaching
sisters as opposed to only sixty-six percent of public
high school teachers had completed four years of college.[50]

However, many questioned the degree of qualitative
improvement actually indicated by these figures. Some
critics pointed to the "superficial scholarship" that under-
lay the indiscriminate pursuit of college credits as a
means of earning state certification, whether or not
courses were beneficial or even relevant to a teacher's
work.[51] In too many cases,

> unity of program, sequence courses, integrated
> learning were all jettisoned so that the edu-
> cational ship might the sooner arrive at the
> port of the desired degree.[52]

Others implied that Catholic institutions were too lax in
granting credits for inferior or improperly done work.[53]

Because the pressure of state accreditation applied
mainly to Catholic high schools, improvements in teaching
standards were slow to reach the elementary schools.[54]
Most college programs were designed to equip teachers for

[50]Schmitz, "The Trend of Teacher Training," p. 348, 350.

[51]Rev. Edward Jordan, "The Evaluation of Credits," CEA
Bulletin 22 (November 1925):496; and Rev. Patrick J. McCormick
"Principles of Educational Reform," CEA Bulletin 18 (November
1921):95.

[52]Meyers, pp. 40-41.

[53]Joseph F. Clancy in a response to "The Evaluation of
Credits," by Edward Jordan, p. 504.

[54]A 1937 NCWC survey found that only 10 dioceses out of
43 required diocesan certification of elementary teachers and
enforcement was not strict. Hagan, "Catholic Teacher Education,"
p. 240.

high school work.[55] Elementary schools were staffed largely
with young and inexperienced sisters just beginning their
careers. Those who showed promise would be encouraged to
pursue college degrees part-time. As these teachers gained
experience and sufficient credentials, they would move up
to high school teaching. This procedure was frequently
criticized. As one critic stated, "to use the parish
elementary school as a stepping stone to the academy or
high school is not good pedagogy."[56]

Critics also attacked the continued reliance on
in-service methods of teacher training, charging that the
imposition of heavy workloads of both teaching and study
on Catholic school teachers had produced neither good
teaching nor worthy scholarship. In 1932 only five of
sixty-six communities surveyed required full pre-service
training for religious.[57] The situation had improved somewhat
by 1940. In a study of sixty communities representing a
little over two-thirds of all teaching sisters in the U.S.,
twelve communities sent sisters to teach immediately
following a canonical year devoted to spiritual formation

---

[55]Of 106 Catholic colleges offering education courses,
only forty-four offered courses specifically in elementary
education. Of 7,871 education students, 6,249 were in
secondary education courses in 1940. Ibid., p. 243.

[56]Ibid., p. 245.

[57]Ibid., p. 240.

with little, if any, pre-service training. Twenty-four communities required one year of pre-service training in either diocesan teachers colleges (8), local four year colleges (5), or in a second novitiate year in the community (11). The remaining twenty-four communities required between two and four years of normal school or college study before sisters began teaching.[58]

One dean of studies in a religious community blamed her community's failure to insist on pre-service training on the continued demand for religious teachers to staff the expanding school system.

> Why can't we stop expanding until we can
> honestly fit our schools with good teachers?
> If only we could stop being credit-crazy and
> give our young Sisters content as well as
> methods, and be done with all this sham. . . .
> If education doesn't make us honest it is
> neither truth nor real education.[59]

A number of Catholic educational leaders, recognizing the plight of religious sisters, suggested that lay persons be hired for an interim to allow religious to pursue full-time study; but pastors, principals, and the hierarchy were reluctant to abandon the most obvious symbol of the Catholic school's religious identity or to pay lay salaries and continued to insist on religious teachers.[60]

---

[58]Meyers, pp. 94-126.

[59]Ibid., p. 98.

[60]See George Johnson, "Secular Teachers," CER 19 (November 1921):559-564; Leonard Faulkner, "Teacher Training for Catholic Secondary Schools," CER 28 (February 1930):77-85; and Rev. Michael J. Larkin, "The Place of the Lay Teacher in Parish Schools," CEA Bulletin 19 (November 1922):234-39. Meyers tells of some pastors who insisted that religious communities themselves should pay the salaries of lay teachers hired to replace sisters studying full-time. p. 117.

Another effect of the drive to secure teacher certification was to promote greater interaction and begin a process of integration within the Catholic community and between Catholics and the educational mainstream. Teacher training programs that brought together members of religious orders representing different class and ethnic backgrounds succeeded to some extent in reducing the educational and cultural isolation of these communities and encourage a sense of united Catholic effort that had not previously existed.[61] A significant number of teachers in Catholic schools, throughout the twenties, despite vociferous objections to the practice, continued to receive formal educational training in state normal schools, public colleges and universities in order to meet state certification requirements. Most Catholic teacher education programs developed in the 1920's were shaped largely by requirements set by the state, and according to critics, offered little positive educational leadership.

> There is a growing awareness among Catholic
> educators that we have been too content in
> the past to adopt an attitude of following
> and have exerted little influence when it
> came to directing the course of education

---

[61] Ellen Marie Kuznicki, "An Ethnic School in American Education: A Study of the Origin, Developments and Merits of the Education System of the Felician Sisters in the Polish American Catholic Schools of Western New York" (Ph.D. dissertation, Kansas State University, 1973). Kuznicki concluded that teacher education programs contributed significantly to the acculturation and Americanization of the Felician Sisters and the Polish American schools that they operated.

> in the United States . . . . It is true
> that we have criticized secular standards
> frequently and complained that they have
> interfered with our freedom of action, but,
> unfortunately, we have no program of our
> own to oppose the secular program and con-
> sequently our attitude has been very largely
> negative.[62]

Indeed, studies showed that specifically Catholic or religious
studies were consistently neglected in the curriculums of
Catholic normal schools and colleges. In 1926 Schmitz found
that only eight of the eighteen normal schools he investi-
gated included courses in religion or religion methods.[63]
The situation appears not to have changed significantly
by 1940 when Meyers found only "a superficial type of
teaching in the field of Catechetics and its cognate results" in the education programs of sixty religious communities. Interviews with students revealed that most
felt their courses not helpful in preparing them to teach
religion. One young nun stated that "if only we could get
the same training in Religion that we get in Child Psychology
I would feel less like a mere public school teacher." A
number of deans complained that too few Catholic universities offered courses in religion for teachers; often when
courses were offered, either they were too advanced for
the needs of sisters or because states did not grant credit
for such courses, sisters were reluctant to enroll.[64]

---

[62]George Johnson, "Dedication," CER 37 (January 1939):5.

[63]Schmitz, The Adjustment of Teacher Training, p. 75.

[64]Meyers, pp. 66, 112, and 125.

Others argued that in accepting secular methods and techniques, Catholics had abandoned their own traditions and compromised the integrity of Catholic schools. Conservative educators were apprehensive about "a shift in standards," noting that "the principles of secular pedagogy and education" were in danger of replacing "those of Catholic doctrine and religious tradition."[65] In this view, Catholic teacher education must guard carefully against any compromise with the ways of the world.

> An educational world whose keynotes are naturalism and materialism can never serve the cause of true education . . . . If in ever so few instances there has been a tendency to compromise with the illogical, godless methods of State institutions; if here and there one detects an infiltration of the muddied waters of secularism into the clear well springs of Catholic truth; if, in a religious, devotion to the higher life does not proceed hand in hand with devotion to higher education, then an appraisal of such education is in order.[66]

At least one group, women in positions of leadership in religious communities, felt that the proper balance between spiritual and professional values in teacher education programs was not being maintained. One provincial voiced the frustrations of many:

> No--I preach the ideal; but the times are such that, in actual practice, we are forced to give teacher-training the major emphasis.

---

[65] Ibid., p. 47.

[66] Very Rev. J. Cronin, Forward to The Education of Sisters by Meyers, pp. xxv-xxvi. Cronin was spiritual director of the Daughters of Charity of Saint Vincent de Paul.

> We cannot retain the young Sisters here
> for a longer period of formation because
> those who seek the Sisters for their schools
> are impatient of any delay we make in
> answering appeals for teachers. We are
> obliged to curtail the religious formative
> period to one year and even during that
> time devote a part of the program to pro-
> fessional training. What else can we do?[67]

Many religious superiors were disturbed when the demands

of studies in addition to teaching led to lapses in the

observance of rules of community life. Others felt higher

education encouraged a false "intellectual pride" anti-

thetical to the proper attitude of a religious. One dean

described the case of

> a brilliant young Nun, one of our best
> college teachers, whom we sent on for higher
> studies. She showed herself, however, en-
> tirely too efficient in arranging her own
> classes, conferring with professors and
> making her own educational plans. She was--
> brilliance and all--promptly withdrawn from
> classes and sent to teach in an obscure
> high school until she learned that religious
> obedience took precedence over all intellec-
> tual pursuit. After three years, she gave
> evidence that she had learned her lesson, and
> is now working for her doctorate at N--(a
> Catholic University) where she is a model
> of religious decorum.[68]

Despite these misgivings, the early wave of resentment

against the standardization movement subsided as most Catholic

educators became convinced that the benefits to the Catholic

system far outweighed any negative effects. In his study

of the influence of standardization on Catholic secondary

---

[67]Meyers, p. 60.

[68]Ibid., p. 85.

education in the United States in 1936, O'Dowd polled
thirty-five Catholic leaders in the field and found that
the majority rated as "highly beneficial" or "beneficial"
state requirements for teacher certification and the
academic and professional training of teachers. One
educator polled remarked,

> I think that teachers have no business in
> a class room if not well prepared. Such
> regulations happily have done more for
> Catholic schools than is generally real-
> ized. Without such regulations, parish
> priests and religious communities would
> under pressure do a lot of contrary things
> which would never be tolerated in the
> name of education.[69]

In conclusion, the church's "solution" to the problems
of teacher education in the 1920's was essentially a pragmatic response "arrived at by expediency, adaptation or
compromise,"[70] and had little to do with a considered
analysis and evaluation of the particular educational
needs of Catholic school teachers. Nevertheless, the
ideal of professionalism had taken firm root in the education of Catholic school teachers.

---

[69]O'Dowd, p. 109.

[70]Meyers, pp. 60-61.

CONCLUSIONS

The broad purpose of this study has been to examine
the rationale and policies guiding the development of Catholic
schooling in the U.S. during a decade of cultural transition
for the U.S. Catholic community after World War I. A combina-
tion of factors in the 1920's including the end of large-scale
immigration and the cultural assimilation of second and third
generation Catholic immigrants, heightened public concern for
social cohesion and conformity, and legislation jeopardizing
the continued existence of U.S. Catholic schools confronted
school leaders with a series of policy questions that would
test some of the Church's most basic educational commitments.
In developing policies with regard to Americanization, federal
funding of education, legislative attempts to extend state
control over private schooling, school standardization, and
teacher certification, Catholic leaders wrestled with fundamental questions concerning the nature and purpose of Catholic
educational separatism, the social and civic responsibilities
of church schools, the authority of church and state in education, and educational standards in Catholic schools. The
resolution of these issues in the 1920's served to orient
the development of Catholic schooling in the twentieth century.

As this study has tried to demonstrate, Catholic school
leaders, in the tradition of "the two spirits of American

Catholicism," characteristically held ambiguous and somewhat contradictory positions on these basic educational issues. While citing the secularism and materialism of American society as justification for the need for separate schools that maintain the unity of religion and education, Catholics unabashedly embraced "Americanism" as a value of Catholic schooling. Though Catholics maintained that the religious functions of Catholic schooling served well the cause of civic responsibility and social order, there was little consensus on the specific implications of Catholic faith for American society. Despite strongly voiced protests against any external interference in the affairs of Catholic schooling, Catholics chose to protect the institutional independence of the schools by recognizing the state's right to set minimal educational standards and voluntarily submitting to independent accreditation procedures. And while articulating a distinctive Catholic philosophy of education based on the "permeation" of religion and education, Catholics accepted public standards in the conduct of Catholic schools that effectively served to distinguish and separate the religious from the secular functions of Catholic schools.

Because of public pressures coming to bear on Catholic schooling in the 1920's, an emerging social vision of the identity of Catholicism and Americanism, and the overriding priority of Catholic leaders to insure the institutional survival of the schools, Catholics, in spite of their ambiguities, resolved these critical educational issues in a way that marked a significant departure from nineteenth century educational patterns. While the creation of parochial schools in the nineteenth century was largely a product of a defensive, siege mentality, there was a decidedly irenic, apologetic mentality operative in the rhetoric and policies shaping the schools in the 1920's. The ideology of Catholic schooling in the 1920's reflected a shift from ethnicity to nationality as a primary source of cultural identification. Catholic schools as a means of cultural isolation gave way to effusive claims for the Americanizing functions of Catholic schools. Preoccupation with the preservation of Catholic faith by maintaining separateness was somewhat modified by a new sense of responsibility to participate in the life of society so as to effect the Christian transformation of the world. From staunch opposition to even limited cooperation with the government in education, Catholics in the 1920's accepted a larger state role in setting educational standards and exercising supervision over the conduct of Catholic schools. Finally, while parochial schools were founded in the nineteenth century primarily as agencies of church education, Catholic schools in the 1920's began functioning explicitly as agencies of public education. The tendency of Catholic schools to imitate the organization, administration, pedagogical methods, curriculum and professional standards of teacher preparation in public schools was extended and reaffirmed in the efforts of Catholic school leaders to demonstrate the educational equivalence of Catholic and public schools.

Several observations can be made about the change process which brought about these shifts in the identity and mission of Catholic schooling in the early part of the twentieth century. First, the primary commitment of educational policy makers in the 1920's was to insuring the institutional survival of Catholic schools. Thus policies were developed largely in reaction to pressures resulting from events and movements from outside the Catholic community. Educational, theological, or philosophical principles and criteria rarely entered policy deliberations as a primary consideration. They served more often than not to legitimate educational positions adopted because of pragmatic rather than ideological reasons. Indeed, for the most part, educational theory had little direct bearing on educational practice in the schools. While the primary function of theory was to articulate a distinctive Catholic philosophy of education which distinguished and differentiated Catholic schools from their public counterparts, in practice, fear that Catholic schools would compare unfavorably with public schools prompted school leaders to pay close attention to and frequently to duplicate educational trends originating in the public sphere. Catholic schools in the twentieth century operated neither in isolation nor ignorance in the wider educational community.

Second, the majority of national educational leaders supported the direction of educational policy in the 1920's, although with varying degrees of enthusiasm. Acceptance of change was generated by the widely perceived need to legitimate the American Catholic identity of the schools, though individuals differed significantly on what that would require of the schools. While conservatives who opposed any compromises with the ways of the world may have won an ideological victory at the turn of the century, their views did not significantly alter the processes of educational adaptation and reform detailed in this study. Some educators accepted change reluctantly as a means of insuring the independence and security of Catholic schools, but remained cautious about accepting only peripheral changes which would not seriously impinge upon the religious responsibilities of the schools. Others actively embraced changes to improve the efficiency and effectiveness of the schools with few serious concerns about diminishing the Catholic character of the schools. Another group of educators shared the priority of conservatives to preserve the unique Catholic identity of the schools at all costs, but advocated educational innovations that, paradoxically, served to model Catholic schooling even more closely along public school lines.

Third, Catholic educational leaders, at least in public, discounted the realities of change and conflict in

developing educational policy. Educators tended to legitimate policies by stressing their faithfulness to Catholic
educational principles and continuity with past educational
patterns. The need for Catholic unity in the face of critical public scrutiny prevented educators from seriously
exploring differences among themselves or from explicitly
recognizing the tensions within the positions they assumed.

This lack of critical self-scrutiny among Catholic
educators was in part a reflection of the church's facile
confidence in its ability to remain above the formative
powers of culture and history. Catholic schooling was
thought to be a "sacred space" in which the unchanging unity
of faith, belief, worship and culture could be maintained,
celebrated and passed on. Institutional changes were viewed
as cultural accidents that had little power to affect the
central, unchanging core of faith or the schools' ability
to carry out the church's educational mission. As Garry
Wills describes, the church

> belonged to no age or clime, but was above
> them all; it had a 'special dispensation' from
> history. History was a thing it did not have
> to undergo. Thus the church could pick and
> choose from any period, odd bits of all the
> ages clinging to her as she swept along, but
> none of them catching her, holding her back;
> she moved free of them all.

This supreme faith in Catholicism's position above
culture allowed school leaders to selectively affirm or
criticize developments outside the church for, in Wills
words,

> what was sound in them the church had always
> possessed, for what the church is, it always
> was, what it could accept now, it could and did
> accept then (that vague 'then' not much explored).[1]

Finally, educational changes in Catholic schools both reflected and contributed to broad social and cultural shifts within the U.S. Catholic community in the early twentieth century. Though the decision to develop a separate system of Catholic schooling as the main agency of the church's religious education task was settled in the nineteenth century without significant challenge till Vatican II, the question of the church's relation to American culture enjoyed a much more dynamic and variable response.

When founded in the nineteenth century, Catholic schools represented a sectarian approach to education. Over against the corrupting influences of a hostile society, church leaders sought to create a distinctive Catholic culture and to socialize individuals into the values, beliefs and ideals of that community. The development of schooling as the primary agency of Catholic education demonstrated a consistent logic, for Catholics understood that effective socialization depended upon their ability to control the cultural milieu within which formal education took place.

However, Catholicism was forced into a sectarian mode as much by cultural diversity within the church as it was

---

[1]Bare Ruined Choirs (Garden City, New York: Doubleday, 1972), pp.

by a hostile dominant culture and Catholicism was divided
into various cultural forms. Because to preserve Catholic
faith in the nineteenth century was to preserve German,
Irish, Polish, Italian, and other forms of cultural Catholicism, schools became organized along ethnic lines, united in
a common faith, but divided by cultural loyalties.

By 1920, American Catholicism, more secure in both
its Catholicism and its Americanism, was prepared to widen
its "churchly" function as the legitimator and arbiter of
culture. The social changes effected by assimilation presented the church with the tantalizing possibility of a
reunited faith and culture. If the realization of this
vision among the entire people was not yet possible; if
America yet needed conversion to fulfill its religious
and moral ideals; Catholics would create a communal life
where faith and culture, nation and church could exist in
mutual support and harmony. This vision of a Catholic
America and an American Catholicism became institutionalized
in the "Catholic ghetto" where the family, parish church
and school, the press, and neighborhood, fraternal and
professional organizations all would serve to sustain
Catholicism in the U.S. as a distinct cultural reality.

The educational counterpart of this social vision
was, appropriately enough, a "permeation theory" of religious education that maintained the inseparability of the
tasks of education in the faith and socialization into the

culture. Catholics' commitment to schooling thus became
an effort to resist the secularization of society and the
consequent privitization of religious faith in a pluralistic, modern world. By the 1920's Catholic schooling functioned
less to keep the world out than to support and nurture a
community that shared a distinctive theological and social
vision.

Nevertheless, the emergence of a cultural paideia
in the 1920's that was both assertively American and thoroughly Catholic imposed new, and often competing demands
on Catholic schools. Catholics for the most part remained
oblivious to the ways in which their appropriation of an
enlarged sense of responsibility for the education of the
public was affecting the schools ability to function as
an agency of religious socialization. Americanization was
systematically undermining the compelling character of
Catholic culture as Catholics became less clearly distinguish-
able from their non-Catholic neighbors. The adoption of
public standards in the conduct of Catholic schools introduced organizational and curricular changes that made
Catholic schools more nearly like public schools and served
to marginalize religion in the curriculum of the schools.
As a result, educators were less content to rely exclusively
on the permeation of religion and education in the atmosphere
of the schools or the formative powers of Catholic culture
to accomplish the task of religious socialization. Many

began to stress the need for more deliberate, intentional and systematic efforts to communicate the faith. Paradoxically, the beginning of specific theoretical attention to the teaching of religion in the 1920's served to reinforce a view of religion as a specialized subject in the curriculum of Catholic schools. While focusing needed attention on religious education, these discussions tended to separate discussions of "catechetics" from broader educational questions and the church's task of religious socialization began to be seen as something separate from its task of public education.

As agencies for the creation of a distinctive American Catholic culture, Catholic schools in the 1920's advanced significantly the demise of the social and cultural separatism of Roman Catholics in the United States. However, the easing of public pressure on Catholic schooling toward the end of the 1920's coupled with mounting public criticism of progressive education in the public schools served to free Catholic educators in the 1930's to more openly question the trend toward accommodation in Catholic schools. In addition, the publication of the papal encyclical "On the Christian Education of Youth" encouraged Catholic educators to examine the distinctively "Catholic" character of the schools. But despite a renewed commitment to a Thomistic philosophy of education as a source of differentiation from "naturalistic" and "progressive" forms of education, the

policy decisions of the 1920's stemming from an apologetic
mentality continued to fundamentally shape educational practice in Catholic schools that were as characteristically
American as they were Catholic.

This analysis of the Americanization of Catholic schooling in the 1920's has particular implications for current
debates between educators in schools and those in parished-
based programs over the most appropriate context for Catholic
religious education. Often, these discussions fail to attend to fundamental questions concerning the nature and purpose of the church's educational mission. On this level,
one might begin to understand these educational models as
representatives of often conflicting understandings about
the manner in which Catholic faith should relate to human
culture. At their best, Catholic schools in the U.S. represent the institutionalization of a public vision of religious
education that takes seriously the need to resist the
privitization of faith in a pluralistic society. They may
also function to isolate and insulate Catholics from significant public problems and concerns. Parish-based models of
faith education may serve to emphasize the radical call
to conversion demanded by a Christian vision of life and
to resist cultural cooptation of the Gospel. They may likewise foster a narrow parochialism or a comfortable civil
piety. The most serious challenge for contemporary Catholic

education is to find adequate contemporary forms by which faith and culture can be engaged in ways which humanize our common social, cultural and political life in a pluralistic society.

SELECTED BIBLIOGRAPHY

Primary Sources

Periodicals

Catholic Educational Association Bulletin.

Catholic Education Review.

Catholic School Journal.

National Catholic Welfare Conference Bulletin.

Books

Deferrari, Roy J., ed. Essays on Catholic Education in
    the United States. Washington, D.C.: Catholic
    University of America, 1942; reprint ed., Freeport,
    New York: Books for Libraries Press, 1969.

_____. ed. Vital Problems of Catholic Education in
    the United States. Washington, D.C.: Catholic
    University of America Press, 1939.

Donnelly, F. P., S.J. Principles of Jesuit Education in
    Practice. New York: P. J. Kenedy & Sons, 1934.

Dunney, Joseph A. "The Parish School": Its Aims, Proce-
    dures, and Problems. New York: Macmillan Co., 1921.

Fellman, David, ed. The Supreme Court and Education.
    New York: Teachers College, Columbia University,
    1960.

Garrison, Winfred E. Catholicism and the American Mind.
    Chicago: Willet, Clark & Colby, 1928.

Guilday, Peter, ed. The National Pastorals of the American
    Hierarchy (1792-1919). Washington, D.C.: National
    Catholic Welfare Council, 1923.

Guthrie, Hunter, S.J. and Walsh, Gerald G., S.J. A
    Philosophical Symposium on American Catholic Education.
    Proceedings of the Seventeenth Annual Convention of
    the Jesuit Philosophical Association of the Eastern
    States. New York: Fordham University Press, 1941.

Hagan, John Raphael. The Diocesan Teachers College: A Study of Its Basic Principles. Washington, D.C.: Catholic University of America Press, 1932.

Higgins, James. Fundamentals of Pedagogy. New York: Macmillan Co., 1923.

Kinsman, Frederick Joseph. Americanism and Catholicism. New York: Longmans, Green & Co., 1924.

Johnson, George. The Curriculum of the Catholic Elementary School: A Discussion of Its Psychological and Social Foundations. Washington, D.C.: Catholic University of America Press, 1919.

Jordan, Edward. Catholicism in Education. New York: Benziger Bros., 1934.

Jordan, Thomas F. The Problem of Vocational Education and the Catholic Secondary School. Washington, D.C.: Catholic University of America Press, 1942.

Kirsch, F. M. Catholic Teacher's Companion. New York: Benziger Bros., 1924.

McCluskey, Neil G., S.J., ed. Catholic Education in America: A Documentary History. New York: Teachers College, Columbia University, 1964.

McGucken, William J., S.J. The Catholic Way in Education. Milwaukee: Bruce Publishing Co., 1934.

_____. The Jesuits and Education. New York: Bruce Publishing Co., 1932.

Moore, John Ferguson. Will America Become Catholic? New York: Harper & Bros., 1931.

National Catholic Welfare Conference. Directory of Catholic Colleges and Schools. Washington, D.C.: National Catholic Welfare Conference, 1921, 1928, 1930 and 1933.

O'Connell, Laurence J. Are Catholic Schools Progressive? St. Louis, Missouri: B. Herder Book Co., 1946.

O'Hara, James H. The Limitations of the Educational Theory of John Dewey. Washington, D.C.: Catholic University of America, 1929.

Oregon School Cases: Complete Record. Baltimore, Maryland: Westminster Press, 1925.

202

Raby, Joseph Mary, Sister. A Critical Study of the New
    Education. Washington, D.C.: Catholic University
    of America, 1932.

Ryan, John A. The Catholic Church and the Citizen. New
    York: Macmillan Co., 1928.

Ryan, John A., and Millar, Moorhouse F. X., S.J. The
    State and the Church. New York: Macmillan Co., 1922.

Sharp, John K. Aims and Methods in Teaching Religion. New
    York: Benziger Bros., 1929.

Shields, Thomas. Philosophy of Education. Washington,
    D.C.: Catholic Education Press, 1921.

Tipple, Bernard M. Alien Rome. Washington, D.C.: Protestant
    Guards, 1924.

Vance, James Scott. Proof of Rome's Political Meddling
    in America. Washington, D.C.: Fellowship Forum,
    1927.

Watson, Thomas Edward. Roman Catholics in America falsi-
    fying history and poisoning the minds of Protestant
    School-children. Thompson, Georgia: Press of the
    Jeffersonian, 1917.

Welsh, Mary Gonzaga, Sister. The Social Philosophy of
    Christian Education. Washington, D.C.: Catholic
    University of America, 1936.

Williams, Michael. Catholicism and the Modern Mind.
    New York: Dial Press, 1928.

Secondary Sources

Periodicals

Abell, Aaron. "Origins of Catholic Social Reform in the
    U.S." Review of Politics 8 (1946):128-34.

Browne, Henry J. "The American Parish School in the Last
    Half-Century." National Catholic Educational
    Association Bulletin 50 (August 1953):323-50.

Buehler, Johannita, Sister. "The Present Status of
    Catholic Education in Illinois." Illinois Catholic
    Historical Review 6 (1924):150-67.

Buetow, Harold. "The Teaching of Education at Catholic University of America, 1889-1966." Catholic Education Review 65 (January 1967):1-20.

Carmody, Charles. "American Catholic Religious Education: From 1776 to the Eve of Vatican II." Listening 11 (Spring 1976):142-60.

Cassidy, Francis P. "Catholic Education in the Third Plenary Council of Baltimore." Catholic Historical Review 34 (1948):257-304.

Cremin, Lawrence A. "The Revolution in American Secondary Education, 1893-1918." Teachers College Record 56 (1955):295-308.

Cross, Robert D. "The Changing Image of the City Among American Catholics." Catholic Historical Review 68 (April 1962):562-75.

_____. "The Origins of the Catholic Parochial Schools in America." American Benedictine Review 16 (1965): 194-209.

Crowly, Francis M. "Catholic Teacher Education." Catholic School Journal 51 (April 1951):118-20.

Curran, C. "American and Catholic: American Catholic Social Ethics, 1880-1965." Thought 52 (March 1977): 50-74.

Dolan, Jay P. "A Critical Period in American Catholicism." Review of Politics 35 (October 1973):523-36.

Ellis, Frederick E. "Aspects of the Relation of the Roman Catholic Church to American Public Education." Forum 19 (November 1954):65-74.

Ellis, John Tracy. "American Catholicism in 1960: An Historical Perspective." American Benedictine Review 11 (March-June 1960):1-20.

Fichter, Joseph H., S.J. "The Americanization of Catholicism." In Roman Catholicism and the American Way of Life. Notre Dame: University of Notre Dame Press, 1960.

Gilbert, John R. "Archbishop Ireland and Thomas Bouquillon: The State's Right to Educate." Catholic Education Review 66 (December 1968):566-91.

Gleason, Philip. "The Crisis of Americanization." In Catholicism in America, pp. 133-53. New York: Harper & Row, 1970.

Greenbaum, William. "America in Search of a New Ideal:
An Essay on the Rise of Pluralism." Harvard Educational Review 44 (August 1974):411-40.

Hennesey, James, S.J. "Roman Catholic Theology in the
United States." Louvain Studies 6 (Spring 1976):11-22.

_____. "Roman Catholicism: The Maryland Tradition."
Thought 51 (September 1976):282-95.

Henthorn, Mary Evangela, Sister. "Foundations of Catholic
Secondary Education in Illinois." Mid-America 6
(1935):145-71.

Howard, Francis W. "Educational Association, the Catholic."
In The Catholic Encyclopedia, pp. 305-306. New
York: Robert Appleton Co., 1909.

Johnson, George. "Monsignor Pace: Educator and Philosopher."
Catholic Education Review 36 (June 1938):328.

Klinkhammer, Marie Carolyn, Sister. "The Blaine Amendment
of 1875: Private Motives for Political Action."
Catholic Historical Review 62 (April 1956):15-49.

_____. "Historical Reasons for the Inception of the
Parochial School System." Catholic Education Review
52 (February 1954):87-96.

Lannie, Vincent P. "Alienation in America: The Immigrant
Catholic and Public Education in pre-Civil War
America." Review of Politics 32 (October 1970):
503-21.

_____. "Catholic Educational Historiography in the
Twentieth Century." Notre Dame, Indiana, n.d.
(Mimeographed.)

_____. "Catholics, Protestants, and Public Education."
In Catholicism in America, pp. 45-57. New York:
Harper & Row, 1970.

_____. "Church and School Triumphant: The Sources of
American Catholic Educational Historiography."
History of Education Quarterly 16 (Summer 1976):131-45.

_____. "The Emergence of Catholic Education in America."
Notre Dame Journal of Education 3 (Winter 1973):297-309.

_____. "Teaching of Values in Public, Sunday, and Catholic Schools: An Historical Perspective." Religious Education 70 (March 1975):115-37.

Lazerson, Marvin. "Understanding American Catholic Educational History." History of Education Quarterly 17 (Fall 1977):297-317.

Lynn, Robert W. "The Uses of History: An Inquiry into the History of American Religious Education." Religious Education 67 (March-April 1972):83-97.

Jorgenson, Lloyd P. "The Oregon School Law of 1922: Passage and Sequel." Catholic Historical Review 54 (October 1968):455-66.

Thomas T. McAvoy. "The American Catholic Minority in the Later Nineteenth Century." Review of Politics 15 (July 1953):275-302.

_____. "Bishop J. L. Spalding and the Catholic Mintority, 1877-1908." Review of Politics 12 (January 1950): 3-19.

_____. "The Catholic Church in the United States Between Two Wars." Review of Politics 4 (October 1942):416-43.

_____. "The Catholic Minority After the Americanist Controversy." Review of Politics 21 (January 1959): 53-82.

_____. "The Philosophers and American Catholic Education." Catholic Education Review 47 (1949):579-85.

_____. "Public Schools vs. Catholic Schools and James McMaster." Review of Politics (January 1966): 19-46.

Murphy, John. "The Contribution of the Human Sciences to the Pedagogy of Thomas E. Shields." Living Light 10 (September 1973):79-87.

O'Brien, David J. "American Catholic Church History: An Assessment." Church History 37 (March 1968):80-94.

Ong, Walter J. "American Catholicism and America." Thought 27 (Winter 1952-53):521-41.

Rossi, Peter H. and Rossi, Alice S. "Some Effects of Parochial School Education in America." Daedalus 90 (September 1961):300-28.

Shields, Vincent. "1911--The Catholic Education Press--
    1961." The Catholic University of America Bulletin
    24 (April 1962):36.

Smith, Timothy L. "Immigrant Social Aspirations and American
    Education, 1880-1930." American Quarterly 21 (1969):
    523-43.

_____. "Religion and Ethnicity in America." American
    Historical Review 83 (December 1978):1155-85.

Tyack, David. "The Kingdom of God and the Common School;
    Protestant Ministers and the Educational Awakening
    in the West." Harvard Educational Review 36 (Fall
    1966):447-69.

_____. "The Perils of Pluralism: The Background of
    the Pierce Case." American Historical Review 74
    (October 1968):74-98.

Walch, Timothy. "Catholic Schoolbooks and American Values:
    The Nineteenth Century Experience." Religious
    Education 73 (September-October 1978):582-91.

Books

Abell, Aaron. American Catholicism and Social Action:
    A Search for Social Justice, 1865-1950. Garden City,
    New Jersey: Hanover House, 1960.

Ahlstrom, Sidney E. A Religious History of the American
    People. Vol. 2. New York: Doubleday & Co., Image
    Books, 1975.

Bailyn, Bernard. Education in the Forming of American
    Society: Needs and Opportunities for Research. New
    York: Vintage Books, 1960.

Barry, Coleman J. The Catholic Church and the German
    Americans. Milwaukee: Bruce Publishing Co., 1953.

Bellah, Robert N. The Broken Covenant: American Civil
    Religion in Time of Trial. New York: Seabury Press,
    Crossroads Brook, 1975.

Billington, Ray. The Protestant Crusade. New York:
    Macmillan Co., 1952.

Bollig, Richard J. History of Catholic Education in
    Kansas, 1836-1932. Washington, D.C.: Catholic
    University of America, 1933.

Broderick, Francis J. Right Reverend New Dealer, John A. Ryan. New York: Macmillan Co., 1963.

Buetow, Harold A. Of Singular Benefit: The Story of Catholic Education in the U.S. New York: Macmillan Co., 1970.

Burns, James A. Catholic Education: A Study of Conditions. New York: Longmans, Green & Co., 1917.

_____. The Growth and Development of the Catholic School System in the United States. New York: Benziger Bros., 1912; reprint ed., New York: Arno Press & The New York Times, 1969.

Butts, R. Freeman, and Cremin, Lawrence. A History of Education in American Culture. New York: Henry Holt & Co., 1953.

Callahan, Raymond E. Education and the Cult of Efficiency. Chicago: University of Chicago Press, 1962.

Commonweal. Catholicism in America. New York: Harcourt, Brace & Co., 1954.

Connaughton, Edward A. A History of Educational Legislation and Administration in the Archdiocese of Cincinnati. Washington, D.C.: Catholic University of America, 1946.

Cremin, Lawrence A. Public Education. New York: Basic Books, 1976.

_____. Traditions of American Education. New York: Basic Books, 1976.

_____. The Transformation of the School: Progressivism in American Education, 1876-1957. New York: Knopf, 1961; reprint ed., New York: Vintage Books, 1964.

Ciesluk, Joseph E. National Parishes in the U.S. Washington, D.C.: Catholic University of America Press, 1944.

Cross, Robert D. The Emergence of Liberal Catholicism in America. Cambridge, Massachusetts: Harvard University Press, 1958; reprint ed., Chicago: Quadrangle Paperback, 1968.

Curran, Robert Emmett. Michael Augustine Corrigan and the Shaping of Conservative Catholicism in America, 1878-1902. New York: Arno Press, 1978.

Curti, Merle. The Social Ideas of American Educators.
New York: Charles Scribner's Sons, 1935; reprint ed.,
Totowa, New Jersey: Littlefield, Adams & Co., 1966.

de Sales, Francis, Brother. The Catholic High School
Curriculum: Its Development and Present Status.
Washington, D.C.: Catholic University of America,
1930.

Dohen, Dorothy. Nationalism and American Catholicism.
New York: Sheed & Ward, 1967.

Dolan, Jay P. Catholic Revivalism: The American Experience,
1830-1900. Notre Dame: University of Notre Dame, 1978.

_____. The Immigrant Church. Baltimore, Maryland:
Johns Hopkins University, 1975.

Ellis, John Tracy. American Catholicism. 2nd ed. Chicago:
University of Chicago Press, 1969.

_____. The Life of James Cardinal Gibbons, Archbishop
of Baltimore, 1834-1921. 2 vols. Milwaukee: Bruce
Publishing Co., 1952.

Friesenham, M. Clarence, Sister. Catholic Secondary Education in the Province of San Antonio. Washington,
D.C.: Catholic University of America, 1930.

Gabert, Glen. In Hoc Signo? A Brief History of Catholic
Parochial Education in America. Port Washington,
New York: Kennikat Press, 1973.

Gallagher, Marie Patrice, Sister. A History of Catholic
Elementary Education in the Diocese of Buffalo, 1847-
1944. Washington, D.C.: Catholic University of
America, 1945.

Gleason, Philip. The Conservative Reformers. Notre Dame:
University of Notre Dame, 1968.

Gleason, Philip, ed. Catholicism in America. New York:
Harper & Row, 1970.

Gorman, Robert. Catholic Apologetic Literature in the
United States, 1784-1858. Washington, D.C.: Catholic
University of America, 1939.

Greely, Andrew. The Catholic Experience. Garden City,
New Jersey: Doubleday & Co., 1967.

Guilday, Peter. A History of the Councils of Baltimore
    (1791-1884). New York: Macmillan Co., 1932.

Halsey, William M. The Survival of American Innocence:
    Catholicism in an Era of Disillusionment, 1920-1940.
    Notre Dame: University of Notre Dame Press, 1980.

Handlin, Oscar. Boston's Immigrants. Cambridge, Massachusetts:
    Harvard University, 1941; reprint ed., New York:
    Atheneum, 1977.

_____. The Uprooted. New York: Grosset & Dunlap, 1951.

Handy, Robert T. A Christian America: Protestant Hopes
    and Historical Realities. New York: Oxford University,
    1971.

Hartmann, Edward. The Movement to Americanize the Immigrant.
    New York: Columbia University, 1958.

Heffernan, Arthur J. A History of Catholic Education in
    Connecticut. Washington, D.C.: Catholic University
    of America, 1937.

Hennesey, James, S.J. The First Council of the Vatican:
    The American Experience. New York: Herder & Herder,
    1963.

Herberg, Will. Protestant, Catholic, Jew. New York:
    Doubleday & Co., 1955.

Higham, John. Strangers in the Land: Patterns of American
    Nativism, 1860-1925. New York: Atheneum, 1969.

Hofstadter, Richard. The Age of Reform. New York:
    Random House, Vintage Books, 1955.

Kaiser, M. L. Development of the Concept and Function of
    the Catholic Elementary School in the American
    Parish. Catholic University of America, 1955.

Kane, John Joseph. Catholic-Protestant Conflicts in
    America. Chicago: Henry Regnery Co., 1957.

Kolesnik, Walter B. and Powers, Edward J., eds. Catholic
    Education, A Book of Readings. New York: McGraw-
    Hill, 1965.

Krug, Edward A. The Shaping of the American High School.
    New York: Harper & Row, 1964.

Lannie, Vincent P. Public Money and Parochial Education:
    Bishop Hughes, Governor Seward and the New York
    School Controversy. Cleveland: Case Western Reserve
    University Press, 1968.

Lee, James Michael. Catholic Education in the Western
    World. Notre Dame: University of Notre Dame Press,
    1967.

McAvoy, Thomas T. The Formation of the American Catholic
    Minority, 1820-1860. Philadelphia: Fortress Press,
    1967.

_____. The Great Crisis in American Catholic History,
    1895-1900. Chicago: Henry Regnery Co., 1957.

_____. History of the Catholic Church in the United
    States. Notre Dame: University of Notre Dame Press,
    1969.

McCluskey, Neil G. Catholic Education Faces Its Future.
    New York: Doubleday & Co., 1968.

_____. Public Schools and Moral Education: The Influence
    of Mann, Harris and Dewey. New York: Columbia Uni-
    versity, 1958.

McCormick, Patrick J. History of Education: A Survey of
    the Development of Educational Theory and Practice
    in Ancient, Medieval, and Modern Times. Washington,
    D.C.: Catholic Education Press, 1953.

Maguire, William P. A. Catholic Secondary Education in
    the Diocese of Brooklyn. Washington, D.C.: Catholic
    University of America, 1932.

Mang, William, C.S.C. The Curriculum of the Catholic High
    School for Boys. Chicago: University of Chicago
    Press, 1941.

Marx, Paul, O.S.B. Virgil Michel and the Liturgical Move-
    ment. Collegeville, Minnesota: Liturgical Press,
    1957.

May, Henry F. The End of American Innocence: A Study of
    the First Years of Our Own Time, 1912-1917. New
    York: Franklin Watts, 1964.

Maynard, Theodore. The Catholic Church and the American
    Idea. New York: Appleton-Century-Crofts, 1953.

Mead, Sidney E. The Nation With the Soul of a Church.
     New York: Harper & Row, Harper Forum Books, 1975.

Merwick, Donna. Boston Priests, 1848-1910: A Study of
     Social and Intellectual Change. Cambridge, Massa-
     chusetts: Harvard University Press, 1973.

Meyers, Bertrande, Sister. The Education of Sisters:
     A Plan for Integrating the Religious, Social, Cultural
     and Professional Training of Sisters. New York:
     Sheed & Ward, 1941.

Neuwien, Reginald A., ed. Catholic Schools in Action:
     The Notre Dame Study of Catholic Elementary and
     Secondary Schools in the United States. Notre Dame,
     Indiana: University of Notre Dame Press, 1966.

Niebuhr, H. Richard. Christ and Culture. New York:
     Harper & Row, 1951; reprint ed., New York: Harper
     Torchbooks, 1956.

_____. The Kingdom of God in America. Chicago:
     Willet, Clark & Co., 1937.

North, William A. Catholic Education in Southern California.
     Washington, D.C.: Catholic University of America, 1936.

O'Brien, David J. American Catholics and Social Reform:
     The New Deal Years. New York: Oxford University
     Press, 1968.

_____. The Renewal of American Catholicism. New York:
     Paulist Press, 1972.

O'Dea, Thomas F. American Catholic Dilemma. New York:
     Sheed & Ward, 1958; reprint ed., New American
     Library, Mentor Omega Books, 1962.

O'Dowd, James T. Standardization and Its Influence on
     Catholic Secondary Education in the United States.
     Washington, D.C.: Catholic University of America
     Press, 1935.

Ong, Walter J., S.J. American Catholic Crossroads.
     New York: Macmillan Co., 1959.

_____. Frontiers in American Catholicism: Essays on
     Ideology and Culture. New York: Macmillan Co., 1936.

Quinn, Mary Antonia, Sister. Religious Instruction in the
     Catholic High School: Its Content and Method from
     the Viewpoint of the Pupil. Washington, D.C.:
     Catholic University of America Press, 1930.

Ravitch, Diane. The Great School Wars, New York City,
1805-1973: A History of the Public Schools as a
Battlefield of Social Change. New York: Basic
Books, Harper Colophon Books, 1974.

Reilly, Daniel Flavian. The School Controversy, 1891-
1893. New York: Arno Press, 1969.

Ryan, Carl J. The Central Catholic High School: Its Origin,
Development and Present Status. Washington, D.C.:
Catholic University of America Press, 1927.

Ryan, John A. Social Doctrine in Action: A Personal History.
New York: Macmillan Co., 1941.

_____. Social Reconstruction. New York: Macmillan
Co., 1920.

Ryan, Mary Perkins. Are Parochial Schools the Answer?
Catholic Education in the Light of the Council.
New York: Holt, Rinehart & Winston, 1963.

Sanders, James. The Education of an Urban Minority:
Catholics in Chicago, 1833-1965. New York: Oxford
University Press, 1977.

Schmitz, Sylvester. The Adjustment of Teacher Training
to Modern Educational Needs: A Comparative Study of
the Professional Preparation of Teachers in Public
and Catholic Elementary and Secondary Schools in the
United States. Atchison, Kansas: Abbey Student
Press, 1932.

Shaughnessy, Gerald. Has the Immigrant Kept the Faith?
New York: Macmillan Co., 1925.

Shaw, Russell, ed. Trends and Issues in Catholic Education.
New York: Citation Press, 1969.

Sheerin, John B. Never Look Back: The Career and Concerns
of John J. Burke. New York: Paulist Press, 1975.

Shields, Currin V. Democracy and Catholicism in America.
New York: McGraw-Hill, 1958.

Spiers, Edward F. The Central Catholic High School: A
Survey of Their History and Status in the United
States. Washington, D.C.: Catholic University of
America Press, 1951.

Stokes, Anson Phelps and Pfeffer, Leo. Church and State
in the United States. New York: Harper & Row, 1964.

Sullivan, Mary Xaveria, Sister. The History of Catholic
Secondary Education in the Archdiocese of Boston.
Washington, D.C.: Catholic University of America
Press, 1946.

Tomasi, Silvano M. Piety and Power: The Role of the
Italian Parishes in the New York Metropolitan Area,
1880-1930. Staten Island, New York: Center for
Migration Studies, 1975.

Tyack, David. The One Best System: A History of American
Urban Education. Cambridge, Massachusetts: Harvard
University Press, 1974.

Van Allen, Rodger. The Commonweal and American Catholicism:
The Magazine, the Movement, the Meaning. Philadelphia:
Fortress Press, 1974.

Voelker, John Martin. The Diocesan Superintendent of
Schools: A Study of the Historical Development and
Functional Status of His Office. Washington, D.C.:
Catholic University of America Press, 1935.

Wakin, Edward and Scheuer, Joseph F. The De-Romanization
of the American Catholic Church. New York: Macmillan
Co., 1966.

Watrin, Rita. The Founding and Development of the Program
of Affiliation of the Catholic University of America:
1912 to 1939. Washington, D.C.: Catholic University
of America Press, 1966.

White Morton. Pragmatism and the American Mind: Essays
and Reviews in Philosophy and Intellectual History.
New York: Oxford University Press, 1973.

Woodward, Irene, S.N.J.M. The Catholic Church: The
United States Experience. New York: Paulist Press,
1979.

Dissertations

Birney, Jane Dominic. "The Development of Departments of
Education in the Catholic Universities and Colleges
in Chicago, 1910-1958." Ph.D. dissertation,
Loyola University of Chicago, 1961.

Bryce, Mary Charles. "The Influence of the Catechism of
the Third Plenary Council of Baltimore on Widely-Used
Elementary Religion Textbooks from its Composition
in 1885 to its 1941 Revision." Ph.D. dissertation,
Catholic University of America, 1970.

Clarke, Stephen James. "Two Schools and Two Ideas: A
    Study of Progressivism and Character Education in
    the Public Schools of the City of Boston, Massachusetts,
    and the Parochial Schools of the Roman Catholic
    Archdiocese of Boston, 1920-1940." Ph.D. disserta-
    tion, Harvard University, 1965.

Doyle, M. Clarissa. "Teacher Education in Catholic Colleges
    and Universities of the United States." Ph.D. disser-
    tation, Fordham University, 1955.

Durkin, Mary Antonia, Sister. "The Preparation of the
    Religious Teacher." Ph.D. dissertation, Catholic
    University of America, 1926.

Ellis, Frederick E. "The Attitude of the Roman Catholic
    Church Towards the Problems of Democratic Freedom
    and American Public Education as Shown in Philosophy,
    the Philosophy of History, and Philosophy of Educa-
    tion." Ph.D. dissertation, Harvard University,
    1950.

Golden, Eugenia Marie, Sister. "Aspects of the Social
    Thought of the NCEA, 1904-1957." Ph.D. dissertation,
    Fordham University, 1958.

Harris, Xavier James, O.F.M. "The Development of the
    Theory of Religious Instruction in American Catholic
    Secondary Schools After 1920." Ph.D. dissertation,
    University of Notre Dame, 1962.

Heard, Etheldreda, Ad. P.P.S., Sister. "A Critical and
    Constructive Study of the Organization, Control and
    Administration of the Teacher-Training Program for
    Religious Teachers in Catholic Elementary Schools."
    Ph.D. dissertation, St. Louis University, 1938.

Kreibich, Rose. "An Evaluation of Curricula in 140
    Catholic Secondary Schools in the Middle West."
    Ph.D. dissertation, St. Louis University, 1938.

Kunkel, Norlene Mary. "Bernard J. McQuaid and Catholic
    Education." Ph.D. dissertation, University of
    Notre Dame, 1974.

Kuznicki, Ellen Marie. "An Ethnic School in American
    Education: A Study of the Origins, Developments and
    Merits of the Educational System of the Felician
    Sisters in the Polish American Catholic Schools of
    Western New York." Ph.D. dissertation, Kansas State
    University, 1973.

Linkh, Richard Michael. "Catholicism and the European Immigrant, 1900-1924: A Chapter in American Catholic Social Thought." Ed.D. dissertation, Teachers College, Columbia University, 1973.

Loffredo, Carmine Anthony. "A History of the Roman Catholic School System in the Archdiocese of Newark, New Jersey, 1900-1965." Ed.D. dissertation, Rutgers University, 1967.

Maher, James Francis. "The Most Reverend James T. O'Dowd, D.D.: Catholic School Administrator." Ed.D. dissertation, Stanford University, 1957.

McCarthy, Joseph. "History of Black Catholic Education in Chicago, 1871-1971." Ph.D. dissertation, Loyola University of Chicago, 1973.

McKeown, Elizabeth. "War and Welfare: A Study of American Catholic Leadership." Ph.D. dissertation, University of Chicago, 1972.

McDonnell, James Michael. "Orestes A. Brownson and Nineteenth Century Education." Ph.D. dissertation, University of Notre Dame, 1975.

Murphy, John Francis. "Thomas Edward Shields: Religious Educator." Ph.D. dissertation, Columbia University, 1971.

O'Brien, Agnes M. "History and Development of Catholic Secondary Education in the Archdiocese of New York." Ph.D. dissertation, Columbia University, 1950.

O'Gorman, Robert T. "The Catholic Church's Educational Mission and Ministry in the U.S.A." Ph.D. dissertation, University of Notre Dame, 1977.

Price, Mary David. "Monsignor George Johnson: His Educational Theory and the Direction of His Influence on Elementary Education." Ph.D. dissertation, St. Louis University, 1962.

Scanlan, William G. "The Development of the American Catholic Diocesan Board of Education, 1884-1966." Ed.D. dissertation, New York University, 1967.

Schuler, Paul Julian. "The Reaction of American Catholics to the Foundations and Early Practices of Progressive Education in the United States, 1892-1917." Ph.D. dissertation, University of Notre Dame, 1971.

Shanabruch, Charles H. "The Catholic Church's Role in the Americanization of Chicago's Immigrants: 1833-1928." 2 vols. Ph.D. dissertation, University of Chicago, 1968.

Sohn, Frederick H. "The Evolution of Catholic Education in the Diocese of Rochester, New York: 1868-1970." Ed.D. dissertation, Indiana University, 1972.

Vidoni, Mary Giovanne, SND, Sister. "Monsignor George Johnson: His Educational Principles and their Application to the Curriculum of the Catholic Schools." M.A. thesis, Catholic University of America, 1952.

Wagener, M. Gabrielene. "A Study of Catholic Opinion on Federal Aid to Education, 1870-1945." Ph.D. dissertation, University of Notre Dame, 1963.

Welch, Constance. "The NCEA: Its Contribution to American Education." Ph.D. dissertation, Stanford University, 1947.

Welch, Cornelius A. "The Growth and Opportunity for Teacher Education in the Catholic Liberal Arts College." Ph.D. dissertation, Cornell University, 1949.

White, James Addison. "The Origins and Growth of the Catholic Summer School of America." Ph.D. dissertation, University of Notre Dame, 1948.

Wohlwend, Mary Verone. "The Educational Principles of Dr. Thomas E. Shields and Their Impact on his Teacher Training Program at the Catholic University of America." Ph.D. dissertation, Catholic University of America, 1968.

The Heritage of
American Catholicisim